RECLAIMING HOME

For the parent who feels life's pace spinning out of control, for the parent who wants to be more intentional with family time but doesn't know where to begin, for the parent who is afraid the years are slipping away, *Reclaiming Home* is your go-to book. Krista Gilbert has packed these pages with practical ideas on incorporating the meaningful into your family's routine. It is simply impossible to read this book and not find some inspiration and ideas you can implement today. *Reclaiming Home* is a solution-driven book to tackling modern parenting's dilemmas.

—**Alexandra Kuykendall**, Specialty Content Editor, MOPS International and author of *The Artist's Daughter: A Memoir,* alexandrakuykendall.com

Krista Gilbert is a woman who pursues deep and intentional relationships with a heart full of love and life! For over 20 years, she has always been someone who pushes me to live fuller, with more of these qualities. When I have been "with" Krista--whether in person or on the phone, reading her blog, or sneaking pages of this book--I feel like I am RECLAIMING who I was designed to be.

—**Eric Scofield**, Chief Development Officer, Young Life

As only the most trusted friends can, Krista grabs readers by both the hand and the heart as she encourages and guides us to find the place where our hearts beat strong: *family*. This is the place where small things, done over time and with intention, carve out the most lasting legacy of a life.

—**Tammy Strait**, author of *Pretty,* graceuncommon.com

This book is a magnificent resource for anyone who longs for deeper connection with family. Engaging and hopeful, Krista Gilbert offers practical tips and wise advise for the most important challenge of all—**reclaiming home**.

—**Kristin Schell**, Founder, The Turquoise Table Community, kristinschell.com

Krista taps into the heart of America by brilliantly capturing the strength and values of the tight-knit family. A compelling read, we are reminded about our critical role as parents in creating a lasting legacy. This legacy will not only impact our own family, but ultimately will contribute to making our communities, and our country, strong.

—**Kevin Parker**, State Representative, Washington's 6th District

No one does intentional family time like Krista Gilbert, and no one expresses herself more clearly, practically and passionately. A mastermind of creativity and purposeful living, Krista's ideas stem from a heart of faith and a belief in family. With her guidance, take a deeper look at how you can make your home beat again with life and love through intentional parenting and planning. Read these pages and regain ground that has been lost. Join her in reclaiming your home.

—**Rebecca Coors**, Mother of 5, Colorado

RECLAIMING HOME
THE FAMILY'S GUIDE FOR
LIFE, LOVE AND LEGACY

KRISTA GILBERT

New York

RECLAIMING HOME
THE FAMILY'S GUIDE FOR LIFE, LOVE AND LEGACY

Published in New York, New York, by Morgan James Publishing. Morgan James and The Entrepreneurial Publisher are trademarks of Morgan James, LLC.
www.MorganJamesPublishing.com

The Morgan James Speakers Group can bring authors to your live event. For more information or to book an event visit The Morgan James Speakers Group at www.TheMorganJamesSpeakersGroup.com.

A free eBook edition is available with the purchase of this print book.

CLEARLY PRINT YOUR NAME ABOVE IN UPPER CASE

Instructions to claim your free eBook edition:
1. Download the BitLit app for Android or iOS
2. Write your name in **UPPER CASE** on the line
3. Use the BitLit app to submit a photo
4. Download your eBook to any device

ISBN 978-1-63047-530-7 paperback
ISBN 978-1-63047-531-4 eBook
Library of Congress Control Number:
2014922139

Cover Design by:
Rachel Lopez
www.r2cdesign.com
and
Crystal Lee
www.newshopdesign.com

Graphics by:
Crystal Lee
New Shop Design

In an effort to support local communities and raise awareness and funds, Morgan James Publishing donates a percentage of all book sales for the life of each book to Habitat for Humanity Peninsula and Greater Williamsburg.

Get involved today, visit
www.MorganJamesBuilds.com

Habitat for Humanity
Peninsula and
Greater Williamsburg
Building Partner

DEDICATION

For my family.
It means everything to me to grow roots with you.

TABLE OF CONTENTS

INTRODUCTION

Four little hands knocked loudly. Grandma swung the front door wide open and welcomed her great-grandchildren into her home, hugging each one tightly. They couldn't wait to see what she had for them. Her house in the retirement complex was tiny compared to what she had enjoyed previously in her life, but no one seemed to notice. Grandma created "home" wherever she went.

The kids giggled as they helped fill her bird feeder and felt important as she gave them jobs to do on her small patio. After their hard work, she brought out the feast. Sandwiches, carrot sticks, crackers, cheese, cookies, and jelly beans adorned the vintage tablecloth. Her mealtime prayer echoed deep roots of gratitude. She was never happier than when her family sat around her table, and we never felt more loved.

This past fall Grandma died. My family and I went to clean out the room where she spent her last days. After fifteen minutes of gathering, all of her belongings were put on a cart and wheeled down the hall.

Her treasured Bible, worn and highlighted, rocked gingerly on top of the snow-white blanket she so masterfully knitted. I said to my sister, "A whole lifetime lived, and all that's left is a cart." But I was wrong. That wasn't all that was left. Grandma had created something far more valuable and lasting than any possession: She gave us a place in our hearts to call *home*.

In college I traveled with a singing group all over the country, and each night we stayed in different houses. I've traveled the world and lived in places with tin roofs and open-air bathrooms. Regardless of structure, size, or geographic location, homes are beautiful because of small actions sown in love—not bricks and mortar.

Just now a delivery driver dropped off a package and asked me what I was writing. After sharing with him the concept of this book, he recounted the hours he spends in his truck thinking about this very subject. Eventually he broke down in tears, describing the brokenness of his family and of the life he dreamed he would live, but is not. He said, "We have ruined our homes in search of success, money, prestige, and significance. Really, the whole time our success and significance have been right under our noses ... but we've missed it. I drive around all day and see kids playing alone, parents gone or distracted by something they deem more important. I never thought I'd get a divorce, but here I am after two decades of chasing empty dreams. It's not the big decisions, you know, it's the little decisions of choosing other pursuits over family day after day. I'm going to look back when I'm ninety and realize I got this whole thing wrong, just like everybody else."

There is truth in his sobering words. We know we don't want to be disconnected from our families, but how do we create something different? There isn't time to date our spouse. Our children are too busy with their activities to have family dinners. The few precious minutes outside of work are eaten up by errands, carpool, and necessary tasks. The electronic device in our teenager's hand blocks any kind of real connection. Our roots seem shallow and vulnerable. Sometimes we feel like a lone tree hit by an avalanche, cascading out of control down a steep precipice. We know what we want, but life and culture moves fast and furious, and we're not sure how to carve time for a solid family life in the midst of such a pace. We simply respond, day after day, to the needs in front of us. But what if we desire to do more than that? What if we want to *create* our homelife purposefully and intentionally? *How* do we construct a place called "home" that allows the heart and soul space to rest and breathe? *How* do we find safety in an often very brutal world?

The answers lie in the reflection staring back at you each morning in the mirror. As a parent, you need to *reclaim your home*. I mean it—*take it back*! It's going to take backbone, daring, determination, doggedness, fortitude, courage, guts, and grit. However you need to reclaim your home, *do it*. Everyone around you will be better for it. Relationships will be restored, families will gather, work ethics will surface, time will slow down, meaningful moments will replace wasted days. Whatever you have to do, it will be worth it. We need to take back our children, take back our kitchens, take back family time, take back our marriages, and take back our lives. Contemporary culture has so much to offer, but we don't have to look far before we realize that it falls short in many areas, especially when it comes to cultivating relationships and honing the skills that were the building blocks of character in past generations.

This book will not attempt to provide a panacea for all of the problems in the world, nor will it even attempt to name them. What it will do is offer practical ideas about how to create your own personal "rooted lifestyle" that builds connectedness with others.

What do I mean by a rooted lifestyle? First of all, I don't mean trying to recreate the agrarian lifestyle of yesteryear. I personally do not live on a farm, nor do I ever foresee living on a farm. A rooted lifestyle does not require acreage in the country, and it can be done in high heels just as easily as in cowboy boots. (I happen to own a pair of cowboy boots, but I bought them at Nordstrom, so they can hardly be considered legitimate country apparel.)

Simply put, a rooted lifestyle means going against the grain of our media-obsessed, fast-food, activity-driven, consumer-oriented, spiritually void, PlayStation-nation culture that has left people relationally lonely and disconnected. Metaphorically it means trading fancy toys that burn out for simple wooden blocks that last for generations.

One aspect of a rooted lifestyle is trading a prepackaged version of life for homemade. "Homemade is best" has become a common mantra around my home. My kids often say this as we are picking apples to turn into applesauce, sleeping under the stars, crafting Christmas gifts, or passing a nutritious meal around the dinner table. There is something about these rooted activities that gets to the heart of who we are. Somehow, in those small actions, life feels real, meaningful, and right.

The good news is that children live a rooted lifestyle naturally, and even the smallest "rooted" activity feeds them as much as their daily bread. They love playing card games around the table, planting their own pot of flowers, reading books snuggled up in a lap, frying a fish they caught themselves, battling with stick swords in the backyard, and listening to tales at the campfire. Children make it easy to live rooted lives if we just create the time and space to make it happen!

Although it may look very different from one family to another, ultimately a rooted lifestyle means living out our values and priorities, building relationships, spending time on those things that bring meaning, and going back to the basics. It's a lifestyle that consistently and intentionally weaves in the small, meaningful actions that make life full and the heart well. Whether you live in mainstream suburban America, rural Montana, or in the middle of downtown Chicago, you can create a rooted lifestyle that is tailor-made for your family.

Just like you, I am in the trenches praying and striving to raise my children in a way that strengthens them, teaches them character, and gives them wings for their future. I am simply sounding the call that most of us are already hearing in our hearts: To run this race called life with some purpose and intention, *and it all begins at home.*

As parents, we have a unique and vital opportunity before us. We have the chance to create and define *home* for our children. This home shapes who they become, how they view the world, and is a foundation on which they stand for life. There is no greater way to impact the world than to influence the children with whom we live on a day-to-day basis. Someday they will go beyond our home, having internalized the values we modeled, and they will make their own mark in the world. It will then be their turn to create *home* for the next generation.

One last note to those overworked and overachieving parents out there: Please don't think of this book as a to-do list that induces guilt, but rather as your own personal toolbox to pull out whenever you need a little help. Many of us are experts in the area of guilt. Unfortunately, that only moves us in a negative direction, both internally and externally. Let's instead reclaim courage and make that the song we sing.

At the end of each chapter, you will discover practical and instantly applicable dares. These suggestions will help you put to action the concepts discussed. Use the book as a workbook. Write in it, scribble your thoughts, and underline those places where your heart is moved toward change. There are chapters designed to help you practically create more room in your life for meaningful moments. Others address *how* to create roots that go deep. If you can, gather some other parents and go through this book as a group, taking time to move through each area slowly and thoughtfully.

You may never have as much influence over your children's lives as you do in *this* moment. So I challenge you to reclaim your home—you *can* change the world by making a difference in the lives of those around you. I dare you to help your family grow deep roots!

Chapter 1

RECLAIMING
YOUR FOUNDATION

The strength of a nation derives from the integrity of the home.
–Confucius

Love begins by taking care of the closest ones— the ones at home.
–Mother Teresa

I n 1956 my grandparents bought a piece of lakefront property in the panhandle of Idaho for $5,000. With the 25 cent floor plan Grandma had bought from *Sunset* magazine in hand, my dad, uncle, and grandpa began to build their dream cabin. For two years they pulled the logs down the steep hill, poured cement, and hammered pine boards to the walls. For the next sixty years the cabin remained exactly the same, down to the wildflower wallpaper, Kelly green carpet, and lights hung low enough to hit everyone on the head. Two years ago, an inspector delivered the news that the logs were rotten from the inside out. The whole cabin had to come down. Because the structure was built before the state-implemented regulations, it was built closer to the lake than is now allowed. The grandfather clause served as its protector. When we designed the replacement cabin with an architect, we only had one requirement—it had to be built on Grandpa's foundation.

All homes are built on foundations, both literally and figuratively. It is the single most important part of a structure, on which everything rests. A properly built foundation provides stability and safety, weathering storms and elements that attempt to dismantle its firm walls.

Our homes are built on foundations of our creation. Every day we are pouring the cement onto which everything else stands.

There are five foundational principles that lay solid ground for any home.

LOVE

Whether we've realized it or not, most of us have probably heard the popular Bible passage, 1 Corinthians 13, read at a wedding. It is the

Bible's definition of love, and it's a good one. It says that love has certain character traits, like kindness, patience, humility, and forgiveness. It also says that when love is present, there is an absence of other traits, such as rudeness, anger, envy, and selfish ambition. It is no mystery why couples want this to be true of their love for one another as they begin their lives together. There is one part of that chapter that I roll over in my mind several times each day. It says, "If I speak with human eloquence and angelic ecstasy but don't love, I'm nothing but the creaking of a rusty gate … if I give everything I own to the poor and even go to the stake to be burned as a martyr, but I don't love, I've gotten nowhere. So no matter what I say, what I believe, and what I do, I'm bankrupt without love." (1 Corinthians 13:1,3, The Message)

Simply put, we can have all manner of activities, dinners, gifts, or teaching within our families, but if there is not love, it will mean nothing. The converse is also true. If there is great love, it doesn't matter much what we do. Love will cause our souls to bloom and draw us close, even if we're simply next to each other eating an ice-cream cone or folding laundry. In fact, it is in these simple acts that love takes deep root.

Certainly as a mother, I make many mistakes. Harsh words, a frustrated, angry spirit, and expectations too high to achieve mar my days. But love humbles me and helps me start over the next day. It prompts me to ask for forgiveness. Love never gives up or stops trying. With the dogged determination of a child learning to ride a bike, love falls and gets up again and again.

Love is the single biggest indicator of whether or not people will feel truly at home in our dwellings. There is mysterious power in love. It draws, beckons, welcomes back, and transforms. The single greatest gift you can offer your family is a tangible, skin-on, fleshed-out definition of love. It will change everything.

ACCEPTANCE

Every human being alive wants to be accepted for who they are. In fact, most of us will go to great lengths to find people who will accept us. I once spoke to a high school student who confided, "The reason I turned to the drug crowd is because I didn't have to pretend with them. I could be who I was and they actually accepted me. It wasn't the drugs I cared about; it was how I felt when I was with them."

I see this phenomenon when my daughter's soccer team is huddled around each other before their games. I see it in a group of women who wear the same brands and order the same drinks at Starbucks. Or in men who cheer for the same football teams. They belong to one another. And that belonging means everything. It signifies that they have traveling companions through life, something of immeasurable value.

Acceptance is foundational in how we view the world and our place in it. It helps answer the age-old questions:

- Who am I?
- What am I made to do?
- Who is for me?
- Am I loved?

When we show acceptance to those within our own homes, they don't have to go looking for it elsewhere.

It is hard to measure this quality, but we can show acceptance in our family by forgiving easily, withholding a judgmental spirit, affirming regularly, celebrating differences, and sharing authentically. Children who feel accepted are freed up to take risks because they know that the outcome does not determine their worth in the eyes of those most valuable to them. Acceptance is a soft landing place when there is a fall. When these practices are in place, home becomes a safe haven.

Communication is a very practical way to foster acceptance. Here are some examples of key phrases that convey approval:

"I see your point. Nice thinking."

"I know you were upset. I forgive you."

"I love you even when you are angry."

"You are great at that. I sure can learn from you."

"I haven't looked at it that way before—very interesting!"

"You are amazing at _____."

"You sure are helpful. Thank you for helping even when I don't ask."

"Would you like my opinion about that?"

"Let me tell you something going on in my life…."

"How do you feel about that?"

"What is your opinion about that?"

"How would you handle that differently next time?"

COMMUNICATION

My son and I are on opposite sides of the communication spectrum. I'm a verbal processor and like to talk through what I'm thinking. I'm also emotional and speak from my heart. Thinking with my right brain comes naturally. My son is quiet, left brained, and logical. His communication happens in his head, not through his mouth. We have the opportunity to work very hard to communicate with one another daily.

Each communication style has its challenges. Too quiet, and nothing gets said. Too loud, and no one listens. Too emotional, and words are reckless. Too logical, and words feel cold. It's no wonder communication tends to be one of the biggest challenges for families!

Healthy communication always begins with listening. Listening communicates care and respect. Become a great question-asker. Refrain from always doing the talking, and instead pose questions that draw people out. Validate ideas and affirm all kinds of news—

happy, discouraging, sad, or exciting. This skill alone will transform communication in your home.

In our family, some of the best discussions about values happen not while we sit and have our family meetings, but while we're hiking. When we are enjoying nature the layers strip away, and windows into my kids' souls open wide. Tweens and teens find it especially useful to be doing something while they talk, rather than uncomfortable face-to-face interactions.

Set up situations for positive communication by including three elements. Consider you and the child as the first two elements. Then, find a third element. This can be shooting baskets, driving, shopping, stacking wood, etc. I once heard it said that boys in particular need this approach. Asking questions and giving the child space to answer freely is an important part of this process. I often remind myself to talk less and listen carefully. It doesn't matter when communication happens, but discussion about family values and truths is an essential element in creating unity as a family.

One way my parents communicated their value of family when I was growing up was by encouraging deep friendships between my siblings and me. They underscored this concept by making family time a priority. To this day, my siblings and I are very close, and family time is still of utmost priority in all of our lives. When we, as parents, communicate a value, and then follow that up with meaningful action, there is an imprint created. This principle is expressed simply in the equation: *communication + action = significant influence.*

When individuals are allowed and encouraged to communicate freely in a home, an invisible circle of connection forms and strengthens bonds for a lifetime—which will see relationships through varied obstacles. Inevitably misunderstandings, hurts, and angry words will occur, but that bond, strengthened through time, sets firm roots that will steady a relationship even in the roughest storm.

PLAY

One of the best wedding gifts we received was a giant treasure-shaped box with a myriad of board games inside. The tag tied to the giant red ribbon read, "Those who play together, stay together." No question, I have found this to be true in our own family. When we take the time to play, laugh, and share experiences, our unity soars. And when we are in a busy season where this is not possible, our unity suffers. Whether it is backyard kickball, camping, Monopoly, or enjoying a ball game on a warm summer night, these kinds of actions create family connection. Laughter and fun draw people together, and break down barriers.

When the weather warms up, our favorite backyard game is "capture the flag." We spend hours chasing each other, and attempting to seize the others' prized bandana that is well hidden somewhere in the yard. Afterwards, we come into the house and everyone lingers in the kitchen, laughing about the games' exploits. It creates a positive tone and climate, and this, in turn, creates a deeper sense of connection and intimacy. Confession: Every once in a while someone ends up in tears over losing the game. We have some competitive ones in our family. Even so, we are still glad we played!

Sometimes families fall into a relational rut they can't seem to escape. The mood is somber and suffocating, and bitter walls divide and sever. This can be especially true in the teen years. Playing together can be especially helpful in this situation, and is a great place to begin moving in a positive direction. Creating fun is such a powerful tool that I've devoted a whole chapter to it later in the book.

The other day my daughter and I had a disagreement and we were having trouble letting go of anger between us. Finally, as she got up to clear her plate from dinner, I ran over and started tickling her. It wasn't a minute later that we threw our arms around each other and exclaimed, "I love you!" We didn't need to talk more; we simply needed to bring some levity to our dark moment. The next time you feel unable to budge in certain aspects of a relationship, instead of trying to rehash issues, begin with fun. When you can increase a feeling of connection, the issues are not as big, and solutions come much easier.

Make a pact with yourself to play every day with your family, even if just for a few minutes. Resolve to keep this pledge and watch what happens.

PRESENCE

"I'll be on a flight tomorrow," said the voice on the other end of the line. My doctor had just put me on strict bed rest, and I sat on the sofa with tears streaming down my face. My husband was in a medical residency where he worked 100+ hours a week, and I had two small children running under foot. I wasn't sure how I was going to manage until I heard the reassuring voice of my father. My dad ran a large business and could not just walk out the door, but that was exactly what he was going to do. To this day I tear up thinking about how he literally set everything aside to answer his daughter's call.

Presence communicates, "I have nothing else I'd rather be doing than being right here with you."

I'm not a TV watcher. Don't ask me about shows or actors because I simply will not be able to contribute to the conversation. However, this past year my daughter watched a TV series at a friend's house and was hooked. She begged me to watch it with her. Now, it's one of "our things." We snuggle up on the couch together and follow the show's latest twists and turns that keep us talking for days. I don't care about the TV program. It's interesting, but that's not why I take the time to watch it. What I do care about is being with my teenage daughter, and if that brings us closer, I'm more than happy to sit on that couch. It costs me sleep and time I could be spending on other things, but there is no doubt in my mind I am doing what is most important: *being present.*

When I was fifteen, I sat cross-legged on the floor. The news had been a blow. A boyfriend, a party, another girl, betrayal. I had enough perspective and self-concept to know that this was not the end of my world, but it still stung. I don't remember much about that situation other than my mom. Sitting quietly beside me, arms slung over my shoulders, was the woman who provided life to me at birth, and strength throughout my years.

These were the same arms that scratched my back at night, cooked meals so that our family could eat together, drove me to countless soccer practices, scribbled out math problems to help me learn tough concepts, and folded bottomless piles of laundry. Day after day my mom used her arms to comfort, build, serve, help, and provide. Eventually she would use those same arms to cradle my own children. I see them swinging from her strong branches as I did, knowing it is safe to hang on a tree deeply rooted.

My mom was not perfect. In fact, now we laugh at some of the stories of her not-so-shining moments. I find these especially funny now that I'm a parent and see the same moments in my mothering journey. Those times when rational thought is dropped at the curb and insanity starts driving the bus. But perfection is not the goal, and it never was. My mom was an exceptional mom because she gave it all she had. She was there. She SHOWED UP. Day after day after day, she provided for each need at hand, whether that was washing sheets or comforting a hurting heart.

Great cathedrals are built by laying one brick at a time. Consider the Notre Dame Cathedral in Paris. It took architects, tailors, sculptors, carpenters, joiners, masons, and glassblowers *100 years* to build that great church. For the first fifty years, it surely didn't look like the great masterpiece it became. But Maurice de Sully, the visionary of the project, knew what he wanted and drove others forward toward that end goal. Likewise, we may not see clear progress as we put effort into our marriage and children and make daily decisions about how to spend time. But make no mistake; a great cathedral is being built. We set a firm foundation when we lay brick upon brick of love, acceptance, communication, play, and presence. That cathedral is what we call *home*.

START NOW

The dares included in each chapter are to help you implement the concepts discussed *immediately* in your home. They are quick and easy exercises that will move you toward growth and change.

LOVE
dares

• Sit eye to eye with someone in your family and ask, "What is something you feel {excited/sad/passionate/happy} about right now?"

• Set out an ice cream sundae bar and ask everyone to talk about the best thing that happened during the week/day.

• Write a heart-felt note in Expo marker on a mirror for someone in your family to find.

• Give everyone in your family a one-minute massage after dinner.

• Welcome each person in your family home with a warm hug and a kind word.

ACCEPTANCE
dares

• Write a word that communicates a unique trait about each person in your family on small rocks. Put them on top of the dinner plates.

• Read about a current event. Ask each person's opinion.

• Pick one person to be in the "hot seat." Everyone says something that makes that person special.

• Select one of the phrases in the acceptance section and designate it as your phrase of the week. Commit to saying it to someone in your family each day this week.

• Find out something new about one of your children's passions. Talk to your child about what you found out.

COMMUNICATION
dares

• Be intentional about being a good listener this week. Make it a point to listen instead of talk.

• Ask everyone in your family this question sometime this week: "Is there anything you need right now?"

• Pay attention to your non-verbal communication. Smile more, have good eye contact when someone else is speaking, and act interested by verbal or physical cues.

• Affirm the emotions shared during the week instead of trying to fix them.

• Share something you are feeling or going through with your family around the dinner table.

P L A Y
dares

• Have a contest to see who can find the funniest joke, comic, or video.

• Hide behind a corner, then jump out and tickle people as they walk by.

• Have a pillow fight.

• Make a homemade treat or milkshakes in the blender.

• Make an obstacle course and race or time each other.

PRESENCE
dares

• Sit beside your kids while they are playing or doing homework.

• When preparing dinner, converse with those around you, or recruit a family member to help prepare the food in order to spend time together.

• Use the morning time to spend a couple of extra minutes snuggling on the couch, eating breakfast together, or sharing an inspirational story or devotional.

• Create a warm environment. Light a candle or fire and play soft music in the background.

• While driving in the car, ask open ended questions like, "If you could change one thing about your day, what would it be?" or "Tell me how you feel about _____."

Chapter 2

RECLAIMING TIME

If you don't have time to do it right,
when will you have time to do it over?
–John Wooden

Time = life. Therefore, waste your time, and waste your life.
Or master your time, and master your life.
–Alan Lakein

S kipping down the hall, the kids were holding out a pile of home movies from their childhood. "Please, can we watch one tonight … *please, Mom?*" Inwardly I groaned. *I have so much to do,* I thought. Work or play? This is a tension I wrestle on a daily basis. After mentally reviewing all of the duties calling for my attention, I looked into their pleading faces. Sighing, I pushed responsibilities aside and decided it was time to play. Laughter filled the room as we all watched younger versions of us talk, interact, and live.

As those faces moved across the screen, my laughter turned to silent, raindrop tears, sliding down my cheeks. A deep ache washed out to the furthest corners of my mom-soul. When did they grow up? Haven't I been with them almost every day of their lives? So, how did I miss it? And why won't time slow down? My daughter, now a young woman, turned and noticed my tear-soaked cheeks. "Mom, what's wrong?" I cried harder. "You grew up," I choked. She laid her head on my shoulder and tears filled those same blue eyes that, not long ago, gazed at me from a newborn blanket.

RECLAIMING OUR TIME

Time. It cannot be caught, bought, or manipulated. It shows no partiality or preference. All of humankind is given the same portion in a day and each gets to decide how it is spent. Grandma used to pat my hand and say, "Don't blink, Honey. Life won't be but a flash." The reality of that statement now rests heavily on my spirit.

Solomon, an ancient sage, said, "A wise person thinks a lot about death, while a fool only thinks about having a good time." (Ecclesiastes 7:4, New Living Translation) I used to read that and scoff. Why would I want to think about dying and be depressed? Now I understand what the writer was attempting to communicate: *perspective*. When I understand that my days are not guaranteed, and that each one is a treasure to be guarded, I use my time differently. I become wise in decision-making.

Reclaiming our homes begins with taking inventory of how we spend our minutes. The sum of those minutes is, after all, how we spend our lives.

In addition to the countless distractions present in our real-life world, there exists yet another one to navigate: the virtual. This second world delivers potentially hundreds of additional spheres to our doorstep to manage, each which competes for our available time. Add to all that kids' activities, work commitments, exercise, cooking, cleaning, and all of the many other responsibilities as a parent, spouse, employee, daughter, and more. It's no wonder we fall into bed exhausted and overworked at the end of each day, unable to identify how exactly we spent our time. But we do know this—there just wasn't enough of it.

There will always be any number of demands beating on our doors to fill our days, but that doesn't mean we should let all of them in. We must peek at each one carefully through the doorway, and then make a decision as to whether or not there is room based on our own defined priorities and values.

Time can exist in the absence of love, but love cannot exist in the absence of time. The minutes we offer another are a gift of immeasurable value, because we are offering something we will never get back.

This thought points toward an element that brings deep fulfillment to our lives: relationships. Even great success outside of the home cannot mask the deep pain of strained or failed relationships inside the home. We need only to look at America's celebrity culture to see that. If relationships are the most important and rewarding part of living, especially within our four walls, then we must take a hard look at how much effort we are investing into them.

Today my husband delivered a gut-wrenching diagnosis to one of his patients. There is a rare, aggressive tumor attacking her body. Like a person panning for gold, she will sift through the next months, choosing only those activities most important to her. I once listened to a talk show where a pastor was asked about what people should do when a loved one is dying. The pastor did not give the answer I was expecting. Instead he said, "Watch very carefully how they live.

In doing so, *you* will learn how to really live." Profound. Essentially he was saying that once a person realizes their time is limited, they live differently, more fully.

For us, we hope that we can learn how to prioritize time without a diagnosis forcing our choices. As we begin the process of reclaiming our time, we first need to identify what merits the best hours of our day and then create a solid list of values that becomes the compass for our decisions.

Next, and just as importantly, we need to pull the weeds. Weeds are wild plants that grow where they are not wanted, and are in competition with cultivated plantings. Plants surrounded by weeds will not root as deeply, as they are robbed of the nutrients they need to be strong and healthy. The same is true for us. We all have those habits sprinkled throughout our days that rob us of investing in our top priorities. The weeds distract and take away from what is important. This process of looking at how we spend our time is simple, but it holds immeasurable value.

My three boys share a room, and there are moments when the entire floor is covered in sports clothes. When I tell them to clean it, they hopelessly writhe around on the floor, because it is too overwhelming to even decide where to begin. One day, instead of coming unglued over the mess, I simply gathered all of the clothes on the floor and put them in a giant pile in the middle of the room. One by one we picked up and put away each article of clothing. That is now the boys' method of choice. While the whole is too much to tackle, reviewing each item one by one is manageable!

As we begin to look at how we choose to use our time, we may feel like writhing on the floor at the big, tangled mess of responsibilities before us. But instead of looking at the whole, we can begin by simply taking one item at a time.

STEP ONE: CLARIFY VALUES

Try the following exercise:

A. **Take a few minutes to settle yourself into a quiet space where you can think.**

Put on some soft instrumental music if you'd like. Close your eyes and go through your last week or month on a mental movie reel. Objectively look at how you spent your time. Withhold judgment and simply assess.

B. **Move through the various important relationships and aspects of your life, and hold up each one.**

When did you feel most content? What was draining? How many authentic, meaningful interactions did you have? How did those come about? What activities wasted time?

C. **Contemplate where you have been neglectful, where you have come alive, and where you need to cut back.**

Listen to the whisperings of your heart as you search for answers. One of the reasons we don't live true to our priorities is because we don't take the time to take a hard look at how we spend our time. We have to know where we are and then where we want to go to arrive at our destination.

D. **Think through the following questions, or get out a journal and write the answers:**

   • What were the highest values in your home of origin? How did people spend their time? How do these values and actions affect how you live now? Are yours the same or different?

   • Do you and your spouse (if married) share the same top priorities? How could you have a discussion about this?

   • What is a value you hold that has been lost in the routine or demands of life?

- What value or activity has taken a priority that shouldn't?
- How have your priorities changed over time?

E. List your top five values.

They should represent what's most important and meaningful to you about life. For example, mine are faith, family, health, personal growth, and fostering community.

This reflective exercise will guide you to evaluate where and how you spend time, and help you clarify what values you want to emphasize. The key to effective time management is defining those underlying values; otherwise you have no criteria by which to make decisions about how to reclaim your time.

STEP TWO: ASSESS TIME

Now it's time to honestly assess how you're spending your time in light of your true priorities.

Next to each value, write what you are currently doing to nurture that area of your life on a daily, weekly, and monthly basis. If the answer is nothing, write that! This isn't the time to be critical, just honest. Use this exercise as a barometer to see where you're spending your time in accordance with your values, and where you are not.

Every few months you may need to revisit this chart. Kids' schedules and life's demands influence the ebb and flow of how much energy can be put toward a given category, or which specific activities you choose to do. For example, our family is currently in a season where sports take up a great deal of our time. For this reason, we are not having as many people over for dinner and socializing. When home, we just want to rest! Normally hosting people frequently would be something I value. For now, using the time on the sidelines at sporting events is one of the ways I am trying to foster community.

Here is my example:

reclaiming time
PRIORITIES

Faith

Daily: Morning prayer, podcast while cleaning

Weekly: Church, bible study group

Monthly:

Family

Daily: After dinner activity, intentional carpool time

Weekly: Family Nights

Monthly: Date night, extended family weekends

Health

Daily: Eating program

Weekly: Exercise 5x a week

Monthly:

Growth

Daily: Writing a book

Weekly: Phone call with editor

Monthly:

Fostering Community

Daily: Reaching out intentionally to at least one person each day with a simple guesture

Weekly: Small group, sidelines at games

Monthly: Once a month fun night

Fill in your own time chart:

reclaiming time
PRIORITIES

Daily:

Weekly:

Monthly:

Daily:

Weekly:

Monthly:

Daily:

Weekly:

Monthly:

Daily:

Weekly:

Monthly:

Daily:

Weekly:

Monthly:

Try not to be discouraged if you have discovered some inconsistencies between your values and how you use your time. Remember to kick out the inner critic and find your courage! There is an African proverb that says, "The best time to plant a tree is twenty years ago; the second best time is *now!*" It is never too late to make a change.

STEP THREE: ADD VALUE

This next step will begin moving you toward that change. Using the same chart, write in what you would like to add so that your life better reflects your values, deciding what trees you'd like to plant. Leave a section blank if you don't feel that anything needs to be added at this time. If your first thought is, "There's no way I can add even one more thing to my schedule!" Don't worry; we'll address how to create room for these items in the next step.

Example:

reclaiming time
TREES TO PLANT

Faith

Daily: Re-start scripture memory

Weekly:

Monthly: Decide on semester service project

Family

Daily: Make sure "couch time" happens w/Erik

Weekly: Game & popcorn night

Monthly: Activity in our area that we never make time for

Health

Daily: Fight boredom by doing a different exercise every day.

Weekly: Exercise with Erik 1 day a week

Monthly: Take the family on an outdoor adventure the last Sunday of every month

Growth

Daily:

Weekly: online tutorial in subject of choice

Monthly: collaborate on a project or activity

Fostering Community

Daily:

Weekly: intentional conversation over coffee or a walk

Monthly: Once a month outdoor movie night

Now it's your turn:

reclaiming time
TREES TO PLANT

Daily:

Weekly:

Monthly:

Daily:

Weekly:

Monthly:

Daily:

Weekly:

Monthly:

Daily:

Weekly:

Monthly:

Daily:

Weekly:

Monthly:

STEP FOUR: WEED

As we all know, in order to add something to our lives, we may need to take something else out. There are only so many hours in a day, and we want those hours to be filled with the most life-giving, meaningful, and important activities as possible. In a garden, weeds rob resources from the plants and prevent them from growing to their potential. Likewise, most of us have *weeds* lurking in our schedules, stealing some of our best minutes.

Weeds may include activities we'd be better off cutting out of our schedule completely, or they may be helpful activities that just need to be limited. For example, spending time on social media is one of my nutrient robbers. On one hand, as a writer in today's publishing world, building and maintaining a virtual platform is a necessity. Yet it is also my responsibility to make sure social media does not devour the best minutes of my day. This weed can rob *hours* of my time.

Periodically I go on a social media fast just to make sure I'm staying healthy. For a long weekend, or even up to a few weeks, I choose to stay off social media completely. I want to control social media, not have it control me. I use a timer to keep track of my time. I don't open certain sites in the morning. This is my most productive time of the day and if I log in, I may not get off! I've also decided that I won't have access to certain apps on my phone so I'm not tempted to be on social media when I'm with my kids. Putting these parameters on my social media use has freed up a significant amount of time in my schedule for more valuable pursuits.

A good friend of mine can spend hours shopping. Thrifty, fashionable, and with an eye bent toward design, she loves the hunt of the perfect purchase. While some of that is needed and wonderful, she talks about how it can become excessive. Hours are spent combing stores rather than pursuing more beneficial pursuits in her life.

Whether it is too much TV, excessive phone use, or browsing Pinterest for hours, each person must decide for herself what needs to go. Most of us can find something to pull out. With your weeds gone, you now have more time to invest in what is lasting and important, sending those roots deep.

Example:

reclaiming time
WEEDS

social media

Stay off social media in mornings.

Put tasks on a timer

Take certain social media off phone

weekly tasks

consolidate all errands to 1 day a week

power clean 1x a day instead of all day long.

Your turn:

STEP FIVE: EVALUATE COMMITMENTS PERIODICALLY

Even after we pull our weeds, we may still want to do more activities than our time permits. How do we choose when we have too many life-giving, meaningful opportunities before us?

I can certainly relate to this dilemma. In high school, I was the kid who wanted to be in every club and not miss a single, exciting school sporting event, concert, dance, or gathering. Not surprisingly, I quickly became exhausted. Seeing signs of fatigue and burnout, my parents sat me down and said compassionately, "You have to choose how you spend your time. You can't do everything well."

The concept of choosing my involvements wisely was a lesson I needed to learn, and I continue to revisit it today. Because of my personality, I've put a specific limit on the number of commitments I will make in a six month period. You may not need to do that, but at least once a year, it is helpful to reexamine those undertakings to which we've said yes. For example, if you are currently serving on the school PTA board, don't sign up again just because that is what you've always done. Really evaluate if that is where you specifically feel led to invest your time in the coming year. I've learned the hard way that if I say yes to everything, what suffers are those things most important to me, particularly my relationships.

Every summer I remind myself about my stated values and pray about where to serve the following year. Without fail, by the end of August I have clear direction. Sometimes the answer means saying no to renewing a commitment; other times I sign up again. The important thing is that I've evaluated it afresh and can say *yes* with joy and excitement. For example, I have been the leader of a girls' group for the past four years. As I evaluated my commitments each year, I had no doubt that I was to continue to be the leader—until last August. It became clear to me that it was time for my exit, and I passed the baton to some younger women. What a joy to watch the girls come to life as they interacted and spent time with these new leaders. When I stepped out, I was also allowing these capable young women to answer a call to leadership of teen girls—a win/win.

Sometimes we will face-plant in the area of time management. This year I committed to some events I was truly excited about, but ultimately couldn't follow through on because of conflicts in my kids' schedules. It was a hard lesson. I've moved into a time of life where I simply cannot say yes to much outside of my family. My children are at ages where their calendars fill up as quickly as mine. That means there isn't much free time left over. This season will pass, but for now, I've learned my boundaries. I invite you to do the same. Carefully evaluate where you want to serve outside of your home and work responsibilities, and then choose wisely. Do not apologize or feel badly about saying no. Rather, shout your no from a mountaintop, knowing that this frees you for a greater yes!

When I was just out of college, I taught English in Costa Rica for a year. While there, I witnessed a wonder of the natural world. Under the full moon, a giant green sea turtle, weighing 700 pounds, came out of the water right in front of me to make the long trek up the sandy beach to lay her eggs. These female turtles were born on that very beach, but had traveled hundreds of miles away by sea to better feeding grounds. Using an internal navigation system, they made their way back "home" to lay their eggs at the very place they were born.

I considered what it took for them to return: persistence, diligence, intelligence, and resolve. Stroke by stroke they moved closer to their destination, every day, moving in the right direction. In addition to the distance, they had to avoid predators who threatened their survival. Then, once they got to the beach, the challenge was not over. Dragging 700 pounds across dry land is unbelievably slow and laborious. As I sat directly in front of a turtle, watching her struggle up the sand, the moonlight aglow on her beautifully massive back, inspiration filled my heart. This wonder of the natural world taught me many lessons.

We often fail to see that the little movements of our lives propel us in a certain direction, and we sometimes find ourselves in a place we don't want to be. Let's decide where we want to go, and then, bit by bit, move toward that goal. Trust your internal navigation system. Like that giant turtle, stay focused on where you are going (your values), avoid predators that attempt to dismantle your mission (your weeds), and pray for the strength to get you "home."

RECLAIMING TIME
dares

• Identify a daily activity that can be cut out altogether.

• Set the timer on an activity that usually consumes a good portion of your day. When the timer goes off, STOP.

• Resolve to spend at least one minute of fully engaged, focused time with each person in your home this week.

• Write down all of your current commitments. Consider each one carefully. Is it time to pass the baton to someone else?

• Identify one person who needs more of your time. Make a plan to incorporate space in your schedule for that relationship.

Chapter 3

RECLAIMING ORDINARY

You'll never change your life until you change something you do daily.
The secret of your success is found in your daily routine.
–John Maxwell

A great building will never stand if you neglect small bricks.
–Ifeanyi Enoch Onuoha

B efore kids, I had plenty of grandiose visions of a sparkling clean house and unscheduled days filled with picnic baskets, hikes, and long family dinners with clinking glasses and flickering candlelight. Reality tumbled these dreams like a washer on the spin cycle after four kids, three of whom are rough and tumble boys, entered my world. Lazy outings at the park turned into days filled with sticky counters, Legos scattered across every square inch of floor, and dishes piled high in the sink. Managing the details of a household is hard work and requires rallying every bit of motivation, skill, and tenacity. Squeezing in home responsibilities alongside work schedules, plus any special needs, can feel like an insurmountable task.

As parents, we have a choice to make. We must decide how we are going to see our assignment of home manager—as an opportunity or a burden. It's our choice, and the answer will set the tone for entire family. All of us have different obstacles and challenges and, as a result, we will manage our homes uniquely. That is the beauty of the human soul. No two are alike because each family possesses a unique combination of personalities, temperaments, and situations. Each one will require tending by the ones who know the needs best—the parents. Sometimes we direct our homes independently, other times we delegate, and at other moments we work alongside. As winds shift, we must adjust our sails through the changes. Every boat needs a captain—especially one who knows the route, and who will show leadership and courage on the journey.

As we embrace responsibility for running our households, what is the goal? It's certainly not to spend all of our time on household tasks. Most would agree that we would like to get the most done in the least amount of time. After all, we want to spend our time on pursuits that strengthen the foundational principles of reclaiming home—love, acceptance, communication, play, and presence. Meaningful time with our spouse, children, and friends, along with fun experiences, do not have to compete with the daily tasks of life in a family. In fact, these very household obligations can be a critical source of sharing, character formation, and team building. Through years of trial and error, I've come to the realization that putting small routines and habits into practice make a huge difference. Small, daily decisions matter. This idea was instilled early on in my life.

The first time I started a D-I-E-T was in third grade. When the naturally thin genetics were passed out, I must have been at the snack bar. I still remember staring at the food diary in the Weight Watchers meeting and wondering if I could write small enough to make all of the words fit. This health challenge has followed me throughout my life. As a competitive athlete in college, I would order salads with cottage cheese while my teammates downed chicken-fried steaks. For as long as I can remember, surveying and preparing food choices has been a large part of daily life.

Looking back, I can say with certainty that I would not be who I am today without that obstacle. Surprisingly, struggling with weight helped to shape my character. It schooled me in self-discipline, restraint, humility, and how to work hard. It also taught me about an overriding principle that has impacted the way I live more than any other: *the power of small decisions.*

This concept can be applied to any area of life, but we are going to focus on our homes and the day-to-day routine. For most of us, the daily chores and responsibilities eat up a significant amount of time. As we study how to reclaim our homes, this is a very practical avenue in which it can happen. Character, both for our children and us, is often built in the daily routine of life. Reality demands that someone cycles the laundry, makes the beds, cleans the kitchen, and picks up the toys on the floor. It isn't glamorous, and that is healthy for our souls. Part of the wondrous journey of parenthood is learning grace-soaked humility, and finding joy in the small things of life. In these very acts a piece of our children's definition of home is formed, and foundational values are reinforced. Our question becomes, how can we improve the efficiency with which we get the dailies done? We want to manage our households well—with excellence even—and find ways to tackle scheduling, chores, and day-to-day routines with prowess.

KICK-STARTING YOUR DAY

From the moment my alarm sounds, I hit the ground running. Like you, there is more to get done in a twenty-four-hour period than I can accomplish. However, by taking a few small steps first thing, I ensure that my morning begins with soul care and focus, setting the tone for the day. Choose three to five tasks you want to make a part of your early morning routine.

Here are my five tasks:

1. **Put on classical or instrumental music.** Music has a calming effect on my soul, and it sets a tone. Since I am not a morning person, music provides a peaceful transition between sleeping and waking, I also like my kids to wake up to that ambiance so I play music in the kitchen, the gathering place.

2. **Spend a few minutes in quiet and reading.** There is receptivity in my spirit first thing in the morning that isn't always present throughout the day. My heart is open to spiritual renewal, and I am able to quietly listen to the whisperings spoken through prayer. I often wrap myself in a blanket and venture outside to a patio chair, where the morning greets me with song birds, or in winter, with a soft fallen snow. Inside, I light a candle and sit in a chair next to the fireplace. At times I read verses from my Bible, other times I simply pray, and other days I read an inspirational book. Sometimes my kids wander down and snuggle next to me, which I love, and the agreement is that they have to quietly do their reading too.

3. **Start a load of laundry and make the bed.** My washer runs every day in this season of parenting, so this gets the process started. I feel better when my bed is made, so that small action makes a difference in my mind-set.

4. **List three things to work on and plan for connection.** In the calm of the morning, I have the mental clarity to prioritize and think through tasks. Writing them down solidifies the plan and reminds me throughout the day what I need to do. I also plan for connection, no matter how small, as this guarantees that I make time to do some heart-to-heart with my family each day.

5. **Include time to exercise.** I've tried to incorporate exercise into many slots of my day, but this is the one that is interruption free. Even if I only have twenty minutes, I do it because *something is better than nothing*!

Make a list of three to five things you'd like to cement into your early morning routine:

1.
2.
3.
4.
5.

EVERYDAY CHAOS

While my morning routine is a welcome quiet, the chaos does follow right behind. Each day holds a full life for this family of six, and part of leading is making sure everyone has the game plan in front of them.

Create a Family Schedule

My ten-year-old son stood staring at the white board with a puzzled look in his face. "Mom, how am I going to get to soccer practice from drums on Wednesday?" He paused. "Okay, I've got it. Here is what I'll do …."

These are regular conversations that we have around the family white board each week. Even though I keep our schedule on my computer, the whole family benefits from having all of our week's events up on the large board. This includes games, field trips, school projects, carpools, appointments, and any other commitments. Family night (more on this later) is also scheduled. When the craved family time is set aside, that slot isn't filled up with other things. If you have younger kids, you may want to use symbols to illustrate activities.

When kids take responsibility for their own activities, everyone benefits. They stay informed on their commitments, and the parents are relieved of the constant reminders. Simultaneously, it teaches organizations skills that benefit kids for a lifetime. As a bonus, when my husband and I communicate better about the logistics of our week, we avoid conflict and misunderstandings.

Parents act as filters in reclaiming the daily schedule. We channel resources where they need to go, and eliminate unnecessary or harmful over commitments. Looking carefully at your schedule is also an opportunity to reinforce your unique family values that you developed in Chapter 2.

Practice Hitching

How many days a week do you stop by the grocery store, go to the gym, or schedule appointments? Putting into practice a concept I call *"hitching"* will save hours each week. Hitching simply means that we organize our time in such a way that we get the maximum benefit out of each day. For example, designating Tuesday as grocery/errand day means that all shopping and errands are "hitched on" to one another that day of the week. This includes the Costco trip, the market list, the library book return, the Home Depot stop for the repair part, etc. If kids are young, consider hiring a babysitter or enlisting the help of friends.

Several hitching ideas are explained below. Some of them can be combined, or omitted during a particular phase of life. Practicing all of them isn't possible, but even implementing a couple will free up time:

Appointment or Volunteer Day: On a specific day every other week, schedule all of the appointments needed—dental, doctor, hair, etc. Try to consolidate the appointments during one part of the day. Again, the goal is to minimize the time spent running around town on errands. On the off week, you may choose to volunteer at the kids' school, at church, or at a nonprofit of choice.

Depending on your work schedule, fitting in appointments can be challenging. Try building them into the lunch hour, or pick one day every six months that you will designate as appointment day, and orchestrate to leave work early.

Connection Day: Pick a day a week that is designated for relationship building. It may mean getting together with other moms while kids play, or meeting someone at a local favorite for lunch, or finally introducing yourself to the neighbor who moved in three weeks ago. On this day, there is a commitment to connection of the heart, which is vital to well being.

If you find it difficult to take time for relationships as you balance work, family and the tasks of life, get creative in combining tasks with connection. Try inviting a friend to one of your child's games, so you can watch and chat at the same time. Cook a meal together, or meet for exercise before work.

Spiritual Renewal Day: This time is designated for spiritual growth. Meet with a prayer group, a Bible study, or attend church. The goal of this set aside time is to deepen roots and to be actively pursuing growth through accountability and learning.

Inspiration can be worked into your busy work day. Listen to MP3s or audio books to and from work. Listen as you exercise. During lunch, pick a quiet place and while you eat your lunch, read, or take a few minutes to journal or pray.

Laundry Day: One method for tackling this monster is to have a particular day on which all laundry in the house is done. The kids bring all soiled clothing to the laundry area, sort it into the designated piles, and wash all day. Sorting and folding are great ways for even young children to contribute to the household. Everyone can work together on laundry.

Another way to tackle laundry is to begin a load at night, then rotate to the dryer first thing in the morning. Begin another load in the morning and switch to the dryer right when you get home.

Exercise: Get up early to work out before the day begins. Walk with a friend and use the hour hitching exercise and connection. Home exercise videos have come far, and are an easy way to fit in a workout in a small amount of time. If you love the gym, try designating gym days, and alternate home workouts and gym workouts.

If you have trouble fitting exercise into your schedule, take a walk together as a family in the evening. This encourages a healthy lifestyle for the whole family and provides connection time, especially if everyone has been apart for work, school, or childcare during the day.

Cleaning Day: Though picking up may happen daily, designate one day a week focused on cleaning surfaces, especially in the main areas of the home—toilets, floors, and bathrooms.

This can be hitched with connection by cleaning in pairs, or enlisting friends to help you. When my sister had young kids, she and a friend blocked out four hours to clean house together. They spent two hours at one house, then the next two hours at the other.

Fun Day: Sometimes we need to build in a fun day to our regular routine. When my kids were younger, we did Friday Fun Day. Sometimes that just meant going for ice cream after lunch, other weeks it meant an all-day field trip.

Remember that little activities can mean as much as big outings. Build fun into your week, even if that means doing something simple, like going to the local donut house and letting your child pick the maple bar with sprinkles. If you are fully engaged in the moment, your child will feel loved, and will have fun.

Over the years, I've done many combinations according to my season of life. The key is to stay flexible.

Here is my example:

Combine these activities:	When:
Exercise + Friends	Morning walks 1-2 days a week
Appointments + Volunteering	Schedule all appointments every other week for the afternoon time slot.
Cleaning + Laundry	Make one day a week the deep clean and laundry day. Get it all done!

Now it is your turn to plan:

List those tasks you do every week, or every other week. Which of those activities can you consolidate, and what day might you be able to accomplish those tasks? Think through your necessary duties and decide what you can hitch together to make the most of your time.

Combine these activities:	When:

When we become more efficient with our time, we create breathing room. This allows time to think clearly about what we would like to accomplish in our homes and the values we want to instill.

KIDS + CHORES

My dad cleared his throat and held a pensive look as he flicked a marshmallow that had fallen from a roasting stick into the embers. "Grandpa was tough," he began, "I'd take a wet rag, wrap it around a brick, and start scrubbing the floor. I'd be there all week if that's what it took for Grandpa to see his reflection." The grandkids stared wide-eyed as they listened to Boppa tell stories of growing up in the family business.

A good work ethic is an essential character building skill to teach our kids. It instills strength, and teaches responsibility that will help make them successful adults. Did this translate with my dad? Absolutely. He is one of the hardest working people I know. This very trait is a significant part of what allowed him to build a successful company later in life.

My parents then passed this value on to us. My siblings and I spent long hours stacking wood, weeding, raking, cleaning, vacuuming, and washing cars. One of the great benefits of chores is that kids learn practical living skills, as well as developing a work ethic. They learn how to hammer nails, fold laundry, take care of a house and yard, and how to contribute for the good of the whole. Chores also teach stewardship. Kids learn to appreciate and take care of what they've been generously given. Most importantly, it gives them ownership in the family unit. Kids who are pitching in around the house are investing themselves in the lives of the people with whom they share a life and home, and this leads to a sense of belonging to something greater, even if they don't appreciate it at the time.

It is easy to say that chores are important for kids. But *when*? Speaking from experience, it is difficult to fit in chores when a child gets older and starts school at 7:30 a.m., has soccer practice, and two hours of homework at night. Creating a doable, regular routine, especially with busy schedules, is the tension. It falls on us, the parent, to be disciplined in this endeavor, and we often are not. We are "too busy," so day after day we surrender to simply doing the work ourselves. Unfortunately our kids pay a price for this. They are robbed of essential character that must be built when they are young. Parents also lose because the workload isn't shared within the home.

Over the years, we have cycled through many, many chore systems. Some have worked extremely well. Others have been epic fails. With each attempt, my mantra has remained: "Something is better than nothing." If all that can be managed is having the kids do dishes with you after dinner, then start there. Have the kids do *something*. No guilt, no sense of failure. Just start. This can be helpful when it feels like setting up an entirely new system is overwhelming. Remember that there are seasons and be okay with that. Kids may complete more chores in the summer, or when they aren't involved in an after-school activity. At other times of the year, reality may require that you scale back their responsibilities. Being flexible helps everyone.

If you are ready to set up a chore system, but just haven't taken the time to do it, here are some ideas to get you started. First, assess your kids' ages and figure out what they can do. Then, adjust your expectations. Your children may not be able to accomplish the tasks like you would, but that isn't the point. We are focusing on what the work is *building into their character*. Let them perform the task to the best of their ability and let go of perfectionism.

This chart is not an exhaustive list, but may help in recognizing what children are capable of and when. Your children may vary in their developmental readiness, but don't be afraid to try out new activities.

2-3 Years

- Help make their own bed
- Rinse dishes
- Put laundry in baskets
- Wipe things down (counters, sinks, etc.)
- Pick up toys
- Help dust
- Sweep (with supervision)

4-5 Years

- Make own bed
- Put away toys
- Set & clear the table
- Feed pet
- Sort laundry
- Sweep or mop
- Help with dinner
- Push a light mop or vacuum
- Wipe down areas
- Dust headboards
- Pick out clothes & get dressed

6-7 Years

- Do the dishes
- Sweep & mop
- Wipe kitchen / bathrooms down
- Put away clothes and shoes
- Sort laundry, fold & put away
- Get dressed & brush teeth
- Take care of pet
- Make bed & keep room clean
- Sort socks
- Help fold laundry
- Weed yard / garden
- Shop vac garage
- Clean up yard and sports items
- Empty trash cans
- Help unload groceries

reclaiming ordinary
CHORES BY AGE

8-10 Years

- Take care of all personal hygiene
- Take out & bring in trash cans
- Organize drawers
- Operate laundry machines
- Help make meals
- Kitchen & dishwasher clean-up
- Take care of room (bed, clothes, toys, books, etc.)
- Pet chores (food, water, poop scoop, clean cages, etc.)
- Organize items, sweep, shop vac in the garage
- Vacuum areas of the house, dust & clean light plates
- Clean bathrooms (mirrors, sinks, toilets, etc.)
- Begin incorporating in family decisions & discussions
- Take dirty sheets off of beds & put back after washing
- Mopping
- Be responsible for school work
- Unload & put groceries away
- Shovel snow

11-13 Years

- ★ Same chores as 8-10 year olds PLUS...
- Organize & plant a garden
- Make a meal independently
- Set own alarm clock
- Do own laundry & help with family's laundry
- Babysit (class at the hospital / Babysitting Certified)
- Mow the lawn
- Be responsible for own schedule

reclaiming ordinary
CHORES BY AGE

14-15 Years

★ Same chores as 11-13 year olds PLUS...
- Wash windows
- Haul heavy material in the yard

16-18 Years

★ Same chores as 14-15 year olds PLUS...
- Gaining work experience
- Heavy yard work
- Maintaining care of a car
- Chopping wood
- Deep cleaning

Chore Chart Ideas

Every person likes a different system when it comes to creating chore charts or boards. If you enter "kids chores" into an online search engine you will find hundreds of ideas and free chart printables. There are even websites that allow kids to keep track of their chores online. This option is our current favorite. There is a place for them to track their points, put in their rewards, and even earn special bonuses.

Ideas:

- When my kids were young, I gave a small list of chores on a post-it note in the morning. When they were done with their work, I rewarded them with Dad Dollars or Mom Money. One night a week we had the "chore store" and they could cash in their loot for a reward: stay up thirty minutes later, play a game of choice with Dad, make an ice cream sundae, go out to breakfast with Mom, etc. Because research has shown that rewarding kids for good behavior works, I make an attempt to incorporate that into our chore routine.

- Keep a chalkboard or whiteboard in a visible place. Write down the chores for the week under each child's name. She can choose to do them all in one day, or one day at a time.

- Use the idea of trading cards as inspiration. Many years back I took pictures of my kids doing various chores, laminated them, and then handed them "chore cards" each day. They each had a pouch that hung around their neck. They put the cards in the pouch as they finished a task, and then turned in the pouch when they were finished with all the cards.

- Create a chore wheel. Have the kids spin the arrow, and whatever it lands on is their chore of the day.

- Make a list of needed chores for the week. Have kids pick one for each day, and choose until the chores are gone. Or "deal" each child a hand of five cards with chores written on each. Those are their tasks to complete for the week.

- **TIP:** Whatever method, I have found that when there is a way to tangibly show completion, it sets the kids up for success. For example, checking boxes off when they are done, signing in to a website to click "done" when completed, or turning in cards. There is a satisfaction that cannot be underestimated in "showing" that they have finished their work.

CONNECTION OPPORTUNITIES IN ROUTINES

Of all the things we desire for our children, connection with their hearts is at the center. We want to know about the scratch on their forehead from a recess fall, the worry about the math test, the joke from the coach at practice, and the drama that ensued as a result of a social media post. These small things make up our kids' lives and to be a part of their journeys, we must take time to know them. The daily, ordinary rhythms of life offer space for that to happen. Driving carpool and nighttime routines are two such places that provide connection opportunities.

Car {pool} Connection

The girls giggled in the backseat and chatted about the latest happenings at school as I drove them to a soccer tournament in Seattle. Turning the music down as discreetly as possible, I leaned back and listened. For the next hour, I gained insight into my daughter's life that I could not have possibly gathered otherwise. I became a background feature as the girls spoke freely about their hurts, embarrassments, and struggles.

Car time. It is a necessity that can be utilized to gain deeper understanding of our kids and promote meaningful relationship. Right now I call my car a second home because I'm in it so much to carpool kids. There are two things that influence how our car time will go: How I greet my kids and how engaged I am in listening.

When my kids climb into the car, I make it a point to smile brightly and show them I am excited to see them. They either greet me back happily or show, by the tone of their voice, that they've had a bad day. This helps me to know how to proceed with asking questions. Teenagers especially can be sensitive to conversation according to their mood, so I take the temperature of my kids first thing. This ritual also requires that I am not on my phone when I pick them up. I do my best to make my calls before they get in the car so that I can be fully present and show them priority.

Riding in a car together allows a natural time for conversation. I ask open-ended questions and then sit back to listen. When my kids are not in a talkative mood, I tell them about my day, or share something going on in my life. My son, Dawson, is a writer and an avid reader. Right now we are listening to his favorite book on audio together when he gets in the car. This is a way to show him that I am interested in what he enjoys. It is not a book I would read otherwise, but knowing the characters and plot gives us a starting place for conversation. As parents, we can learn to appreciate what our children care about because of our love for them!

Driving carpool is a natural way to get to know our children's friends. As parents we want to know the character and personalities of the people with whom they are choosing to associate. I learn so much by asking questions and listening to the conversations that happen during carpool. I also am able to see the dynamic of the friendship, which is very helpful as we coach our kids in navigating relationships.

On one trip with my daughter, we also listened to an audio book that we were both excited to read on our way to and from the destination. We could hardly wait to get in the car to see what happened next in the story. It also gave us something fun to talk about while we were together. Car time is a natural opportunity to promote connection.

After-Dinner Connection

Finding individual moments with family members can be difficult, yet relationships thrive under that focused attention. Even if we can't create large amounts of time, we can seek out little windows of opportunity during the regular routine of life. The time between dinner and bedtime is set up perfectly for this individual heart connection. In many families, people disperse to several areas of the house to work on homework, read, play, or watch a game. During this window, my husband and I practice "couch time" while the kids clean up from dinner. Couch time is exactly what it sounds like; we sit on the couch and talk about our day for fifteen to twenty minutes. Having a daily "check in" helps with connection and communication about what is going on in our lives.

After that space with my husband, I often make rounds, checking in on each child. For example, I begin in the kitchen, helping whoever is at the kitchen island doing homework. After a while, I venture to find another playing Legos. I offer to play for a few minutes. This is a time for quick and easy connection, nothing elaborate. When my daughter was overwhelmed with massive loads of homework during one particular year, I would go into the office and sit in there while she studied. We didn't talk at all, but I was present. It was surprising the difference this made in our relationship.

For many years, we designated one day of the week for each child. On that day, he helped with dinner and organized meal clean up, but more importantly, he got to do something special after dinner with Dad. It was scheduled connection and it made a difference.

Bedtime Connection

My brother, Mitch, and his wife, Sarah, are masters of using the daily routine to promote connection and ritual. Both are wildly talented actors and musicians. The bedtime routine in their household is full of melodic ballads, books read with lively impersonations, and fanciful stories. This one ritual has already created deep roots in the lives of their children.

Bedtime is a sacred slot at the end of the day when all are tucked into bed and the lights are low. Voices whisper and quiet envelopes the house. This vulnerable space lends itself to heart-to-heart sharing when we take the time to sit in the shadows with our children. If you have young children, the going-to-bed routine may seem more like a power struggle than a welcome connection. But over time, ritual and routine can create a positive pattern at bedtime. With older kids, tired from a day bursting with activity, some nights I want to rush everyone off to bed, say a quick prayer, and close the door. In doing so, I miss an opportunity for deeper connection.

I come from a strong tradition of back-scratching and my kids are no exception. Sometimes the best conversations happen while I am scratching their backs. Healthy physical touch is important to kids. Young children naturally spend time hugging, crawling into laps, and holding hands. As they grow older, physical touch doesn't come as easily. This is especially true in the teen years, and parents often shy away from this important connector. Fathers and daughters can struggle with this as girls enter adolescence and start to look more like young women. Bedtime is a natural way for this healthy touch to happen with hugs, back-scratches, and kisses on the forehead.

Bedtime is also a great way to create important rituals that give kids security and comfort. At our house I tell the younger ones stories about "Big Bad Bird." He is a bird who is always getting into trouble with the other birds in town by pulling pranks. The kids laugh as they follow his shenanigans, but there is usually a redeeming part to the story. Either Big Bad Bird learns his lesson, or someone shows him a moving act of mercy or friendship. I see the security that these silly stories bring as my kids smile and close their eyes to go to sleep, satisfied with the ending.

When my sister and I are together at family gatherings, we masquerade as the "Bubblegum Sisters." This goofy duo tucks in the cousins with Valley-girl type stories of how they used gum for all sorts of crazy uses throughout the day. They use it to fish, cross bridges, and even to fly. The kids love the impersonation, and yell as if they have discovered a great secret, "*We know who you are Bubblegum Sisters!*"

Though the progression of bedtime rituals change throughout a child's life, this time provides solid roots at every age.

Ideas for younger kids:

- Read chapter books out loud
- Form a back-scratch train
- Sing songs
- Create make-believe stories together
- Brush hair
- Give a foot rub
- Stargaze
- Wish on a star
- Pray

Ideas for older kids:

- Read a classic out loud
- Spell words on their backs and have them guess what it says
- Massage their backs for a few minutes
- Sit in their room and help them pick up while you talk
- Listen to music together
- Talk about highs and lows
- Quiz them on homework
- Ask questions and let them talk
- Bring in a hot drink and sit with them while they enjoy it

Daily rituals are opportunities for connection when we approach them with that intention in mind.

The Busy Parent's Letter to the World

BE WARNED:
We are loud. And messy. And even a bit wild.
There are shoes on the floor, the toilets aren't always scrubbed, and the laundry is backed up. There may be fighting and definitely yelling.

But please come in.

This is our crazy – what we call family.
And within that chaos, we are sure that bursting out of the seeds of that imperfection will sprout people who learn how to honor one another, work hard, and live with passion.

HOW?

Because we plant in the soil of deep love, persevering spirits, authentic living, and prayer.
It doesn't look like it now – the seeds are barely sprouting and even some days look as if they might wilt.
But make no mistake. The harvest will come.

Because we do not give up.

So come on in. Suspend judgment.
Tread carefully so as not to step on the seedlings, and join me in watering this beautiful garden.

RECLAIMING ORDINARY
dares

• Think through your day. What two tasks can you combine together?

• What chore can you have your children do today?

• Turn off your phone while you are in the car. Make an effort to engage your children.

• Choose a place you can put a whiteboard or chalkboard to write important family activities.

• When you get up tomorrow morning, commit to doing one thing to start your day off right.

Chapter 4

RECLAIMING MARRIAGE

The happy state of matrimony is, undoubtedly, the surest and most lasting foundation of comfort and love … the cause of all good order in the world, and what alone preserves it from the utmost confusion.
—Benjamin Franklin

A successful marriage is an edifice that must be rebuilt every day.
—Andre Maurois

R ain pounded the windowpane. Drops slid down the glass in a zigzag pattern, reflecting the current of my heart. I was committed to my marriage, but I was tired of feeling like we were living separate lives … I was lonely and sad. A dear friend, Rebecca, sat with me in my grief, reading a scripture from the book of Isaiah at her kitchen table, while tiny hands ran matchbox cars over our feet.

Work had become all-consuming for my husband and motherhood had enveloped me. We did our jobs well, but independently. The distance spurred a desire to run into my own self and needs and away from him—the exact opposite of what would heal us.

Engrossed in the me-culture in which we live, I struggled through many cultural messages that supported happiness and satisfaction over faithfulness and perseverance. But I knew better than to look to culture for answers to my problems. Solid family examples had shown me over years what it looks like to press into challenging circumstances with grit and determination. You communicate openly, invest more time, not less, pull back from those things that take away from the marriage, and never, ever give up. So that's what we did. I also had a community around me that picked me up, bandaged some wounds, and then sent me back onto the field to fight harder for my marriage—to run into the game, not away from it. A winning team does that.

A wedding ring diamond is a beautiful symbol of the purifying process hammered out on the anvil of marriage. Diamonds are crystals of pure carbon forged in the inner layers of the earth under extreme pressure and heat. That harsh combination causes each carbon atom to adhere to four other carbon atoms, making the diamond remarkably strong. Out of that hostile environment comes the gem that is valuable, durable, and stunning enough to represent marriage itself.

Marriage is a lot like the forging of a diamond. Heat and pressure will come. In fact, it is a necessary and important part of the relationship formation process. Without it, there is no treasure. The temptation to flee the discomfort will be great, and might sometimes be the easier choice. But if we stay and bind ourselves to the one to whom we whispered a promise, we come out like that carbon atom—stronger, wiser, and more beautiful than before.

Just to be clear: To those of you in abusive or unethical situations, this does not apply. Many are in marital crisis that are beyond the scope of what I am discussing here. But to the rest of us—to the ones who have just grown weary, contemptuous, distant, tired, and bored—we can choose to invite the refining process, to hang on, knowing that it leads to something greater.

More than a decade after that day at my friend's table, almost twenty years in, we're seeing the sparkle on our gem. We still have struggles in our relationship, but the struggles don't crack our foundation anymore. Our love is deeper and more real. It is not a fleeting feeling, but a resolved decision of grit that has been forged over countless moments of tears, arguments, conversations, experiences, prayers, and laughter. We have risen to mountaintops and sunk to valleys. And we've done it, arm and arm, together. That counts for something in this life.

The decision to declare, "I do" to each other involves commitment. Even when it's hard. Even when unexpected difficulties emerge. Even when the other person sometimes disappoints. There is no trading in for a newer model. Because love is less about the happiness we're hoping to receive and more about the decisions we make to offer patience, kindness, joy, and forgiveness to our life partner *every single day*.

Reclaiming marriage is an active choice. Reclaiming means that we refuse to give up when we encounter bitterness, contempt, disregard, or neglect. It means we fight *for* our marriages rather than *against* them. One of my favorite sayings of Jesus reflects this stance, "Every kingdom divided against itself will be ruined, and every city or household divided against itself will not stand." (Matthew 12:25, New International Version) There are countless examples of the power of unity in history, in sports team legends, and in businesses. Our marriages are no exception. We cannot be divided and expect that our families will not suffer. They will. Deeply. It is worth our best effort to be unified—both for our own sake and for the sake of our children. Let's make a decision to stand—firmly, with an unshakeable resolve.

Have you ever been to one of those water parks where a giant bucket fills with water at the top of a large structure? People stand underneath and wait until the bucket suddenly gets to a tipping point and spills the entire tidal wave onto their heads. Marriage is a lot like that bucket. Every day we fill our marital buckets with either fresh, life-giving water, or with polluted dregs. Often we are much more likely to deposit positive affirmations into our children's or friend's buckets than we are to our spouse's. It's important to recognize that we often take our spouse for granted, and our deposits are sometimes sparse or negative. Here is the truth that we sometimes don't want to admit: *We get to choose what goes into our buckets.*

Healthy people in life-giving marriages know and live by certain truths that fill their buckets with living water. Many of these truths echo the same principles for a strong family foundation, lived out in the marriage relationship: love, acceptance, communication, play, and presence. Here are some truths that will help you reclaim health and unity in your own marriage, allowing for deep roots to grow:

MY SPOUSE IS NOT RESPONSIBLE TO COMPLETE ME

I can be a healthy, whole person on my own. While my spouse profoundly adds to my life, I do not look to my spouse to fill me. When the pressure of my happiness is on another human being, I set up the relationship for disappointment, pain, and resentment. The responsibility for my well-being is mine alone and I accept it.

In those areas of my life that are unhealthy, as a result of patterns set by my family of origin, or from my own poor choices, today I can choose to get help. I will begin by telling myself the truth about why I am unhealthy—what the real reason is for my repeated behavior. This requires the courage to be vulnerable with myself. Then, I will accept responsibility for my own well-being and seek the help I need. In doing so, I will come to my marriage as a healthier person and this will yield a marriage that reflects health rather than sickness.

LOVE IS A DECISION, NOT A FEELING

Deep, soulful, sacrificial love is a series of decisions made in the everyday workings of life. No one can make you love someone. It is your choice whether or not you love. In the initial infatuation period of a relationship, feelings flow as gracefully as a gentle breeze. Overlooking faults is easy, attraction sizzles, and dreams of a bright future dominate conversation. But experts agree that the honeymoon phase only lasts about eighteen months to two years. At some point, everyone comes off of that mountaintop experience. It is then that the choosing begins.

Every day we make decisions toward our marriage, or away from it. Marriage is not static. As most couples learn, we are in a process of continually narrowing the gap toward intimacy, or widening the chasm.

Falling in and out of love has become an accepted concept in our culture—as if we have no control over it at all, and are not responsible for our heart decisions. That is simply not the case. It doesn't mean love will be easy, or that the other person will even receive our love, but we do control whether or not we choose to act in a loving way. When we change what we do, it changes how we feel.

Love is choosing to speak a kind word, refraining from speaking an unkind one, and accepting who the other person is rather than demanding they be someone else. Sometimes it may even be as simple and practical as getting off the couch to get a glass of water for the other to demonstrate thoughtfulness. All of these require that we put another's needs before our own.

One of the main obstacles holding us captive is our own selfishness. There are times when we are so focused on our desires that we are blind to our spouse's. We all share this selfish tendency—it's human nature. Marriage is one of the prime opportunities we have in this life to fight against selfishness. It's good for our souls to have to pin this monster to the mat. When we are the center of our universe, when everything revolves around our rights, our needs, our ways, our viewpoints, and our desires, we have the potential to become very unhealthy. This narcissistic lifestyle breeds discontent and failed relationships.

Accompanying this self-focus are feelings that may lead us astray. While feelings are very real, we also need to realize that they are fleeting and not always accurate. There are many mornings I don't feel like exercising, but I know that my body needs it to be healthy and that ultimately I'll be better for it mentally and physically. The same is true with relationships. When we decide to honor the commitment we made and move toward our spouse, *even when we don't feel like it*, we are filling our bucket with life-giving water. And the bonus? Our feelings follow. I once heard a speaker quote, "Feelings are great followers, and very bad leaders."

MOVE CHILDREN OUT OF THE CENTER

This may sound strange, but one of the greatest threats to a marriage can be a couple's children. How is this possible? The kids take center stage to the neglect of the marital relationship. I have struggled with this endlessly in our own marriage in different ways.

When my children were young, I was just tired all of the time. I was a stay-at-home mom without family nearby, and my husband worked a lot. That meant I was on twenty-four-hour duty with no breaks. I didn't want anyone else to need me or require anything from me. So my kids got the best of me, and when my husband got home, there wasn't much left over.

Now that my kids are older, I find that they still need me, but differently. I often spend hours running them places, or waiting patiently for them to get to a place in our conversation where they open up to me. Also, now they have so many activities, games, and commitments that it doesn't leave much room for marital romance. If we try to leave for a get-away weekend, I know that I'm leaving their caretaker with four-kid chaos, and relinquishing that control often prevents me from leaving at all.

Ultimately, there is never a good time in the season of parenting to cultivate our marriages, and yet, *it simply cannot wait.* Anything not tended to dies of neglect. We don't want to wake up in the empty nest and see a stranger sharing our home.

We can counter the tendency to put our children in the center by consciously choosing to put our marriage first.

How do we actually put our marriages first on a daily basis? It's difficult and takes intention. For some that may mean going on a date once a week, for others it will be having conversation every day over coffee before work, and for others it may be showing affection with lots of hugs and hand holding. The particular action isn't as important as the regular choice to connect.

One of the main ways we put children first is by siding with our kids during conflict rather than our spouse. A unified team is important, and this undermines the very foundation of it. This does not mean that there won't be times when we disagree with a decision our spouse has made. Of course we will. But we can still remain unified during these moments. Behind closed doors, away from the children, we can talk about it, hash it out, and then return to the family in agreement. Sometimes we may need to swallow and decide to let go in order to compromise. It is important for the children to see that there is mutual respect and that they can't play one parent against the other.

If you are navigating a blended family, this gets even more complicated. One parent can feel a certain amount of loyalty to protect the needs of his or her own children. That child or those children become the center of one parent's circle, but not the other. That dynamic fosters division, where the spouse feels that he or she is in competition with the children. In conflict then, the spouse does not feel chosen, but sided against. Try to stay focused on the team approach. Let both the children and stepchildren see that you make decisions together, and tackle complicated issues as a team.

MAKE FORGIVENESS A DAILY RHYTHM

Keeping short accounts is one of the best ways to keep a relationship healthy. Building up resentment over a long period of time breeds damaging anger and bitterness that slowly dries up a marriage. A hardened heart is the real danger in resentment. Love is difficult to grow in a parched soul.

Understanding the essence of forgiveness may help us adopt this as a lifestyle. Forgiveness simply means that we choose to give up our right to punish the other person for their behavior. It does not mean we don't discuss it thoroughly or work through a plan for change—these steps are healthy. It does mean that we offer grace, even when it is undeserved. Because marriage is a relationship between two imperfect people who often mess up and hurt each other, we know that we will be the ones on the other end of forgiveness before too long. Some offenses are more hurtful than others, but in the long run, choosing to forgive benefits everyone—you, your spouse, and your family.

Forgiveness rejuvenates your marriage with buckets of fresh water. If you are unsure of how to move from resentment toward forgiveness begin with these three steps:

- Acknowledge the full weight of the pain. Allow yourself to dig deeply to the core of why the relationship or offense hurt so badly and profoundly.

- Then … breathe as I say this … let go of your anger. Do something tangible to symbolize your letting go—burn a piece of paper with the offense written on it, let go of balloons, or write the offense on a rock and bury it in the ground.

- You are choosing to drink fresh water rather than poison by setting the resentment free. That builds strength. Write in a journal or in a letter to a close friend how you have grown because of the experience and how the future will be different because of what you've learned. Look for redeeming threads in your story and tell others about it.

SEX HAS POWER

When a friend comes to me with marital problems, one of the first questions I ask is, "How often are you having sex?" This may seem intrusive, but it is a key indicator of how severe the problems are in the relationship. Show me a couple who doesn't have sex on a regular to semi-regular basis, and I'll show you a marriage that is in grave danger. It is an indicator. Why? This union of our bodies has a mysterious and profound impact on our emotional connection. This statement is presuming a relationship not based on abuse of sexual power, in which case you need to seek outside help.

It does not take a sex-expert to know the positive impact that coming together physically can have on a marriage. I've lived it. There is a humility and acceptance in this vulnerable act that, along with the chemical reaction in the body, creates an invisible bond. Sex transforms us from roommates running a family to lovers. It pushes complacency aside and beckons the passion we so desire. We may need sex for different reasons, but whether male or female, sex is one of the best ways to invite intimacy and health into our marriages. Bottom line—make time for physical intimacy, it fills your bucket.

PEOPLE INFLUENCE

Most of us have many acquaintances, but there are only a few who make up our close circle, our team. To this group we give permission to influence. How does your team feel about your marriage? Do they move you toward it or away from it? What activities are common to this group, and do they support or tear down the values in your primary relationship? Sometimes we find allies who will side with us in destructive behaviors, and who help us find ways to rationalize them. What we really need are bold cheerleaders—those who will listen to our hearts, and then help us find ways to pour refreshing water on our marriages.

Some people don't have a team. If you find yourself in this category, think through the kind of people you'd like to have cheering you on. What kinds of values do they hold? Do they value marriage? Are they committed to building up the marriages around them? Begin by regularly inviting couples into your home to share a meal. Be persistent until you find those people who exert positive influence.

KINDNESS IS KING

Kindness is the language which the
deaf can hear and the blind can see.
–Mark Twain

Sincere kindness opens hearts, offers dignity, and builds trust. It is something that is hard to define, but easy to identify. We know when we are in the presence of kindness, and when we are not. A kind person shows thoughtfulness, humility, gentleness, care, and patience both in actions and in words spoken. What marriage could not use more of these? This is one area in particular where small counts. It is often the almost unnoticed acts that create the most lasting impact.

I have a very close friend who exudes kindness. Because we grew up together, I have watched her interact with hundreds of people over many years. People love Katie in a way that is unusual. They *adore* her. Growing up I was the more outgoing, gregarious part of our duo. There was no doubt I was, outwardly, the leader. But Katie led also, just quietly and differently, by example. She shined so brightly that there was no mistaking that she was special. In my adult life I finally put a finger on what makes her so very rare. There is one trait she possesses that stands up and shouts above all the rest. It is this very characteristic that has allowed her to be full of kindness. What is her secret? Katie speaks positively; *she lacks a critical spirit.*

A critical spirit focuses on the negative in a person, often nitpicking and pointing fingers. It keeps a record of wrongs and often punishes as a result. In a marriage this destroys respect and good will. There have been seasons where I found myself cultivating negativity, and our marriage reflected that attitude. It's not a fun place to be, for anyone, and it is a ruthless destroyer of the growth of our relationship.

Sometimes it helps to picture a truly kind person in your head and think through how he or she shows that specifically. Adapt the actions to fit your personality, but this will give you a starting place if it isn't a natural habit. Begin or ramp up practicing daily movements of kindness in your home and watch the transformation of the tone in your marriage. The key is to practice kindness *every day.*

BELIEVE THE BEST

Teaming up with a critical spirit is an attitude of judgment. When hurt or angry, it is common for a person to believe the worst about the one with whom they are experiencing conflict. We spin motivations and intentions around in our heads until we are sure there wasn't even an ounce of good in the other person. This is our emotion shouting over reasonable thought. Though there is always an exception to the rule, for most couples, spouses do not intentionally choose ill will toward their spouse. Sure, they can be thoughtless, or make significant mistakes, but more often than not, it's just that—an error. Why is it we are so quick to give ourselves the benefit of the doubt but not others? Seeing from another's perspective is a gift of immeasurable value. It is also wisdom.

Consider what would happen if you began to think the best about your spouse and their intentions. Defenses would fall, hearts would unify, and conflict would decrease. Let's treat our spouse with the same consideration we want in return, it will go a long ways toward refilling the bucket of refreshment in our marriage.

FUN IS INDISPENSABLE

People are simply happier when there is fun in the home and in relationships. Unfortunately, this is one of the first things to go when there is conflict or when schedules are busy and stresses mount. We know we need fun, but don't create space for it. Would it change your mind if you knew that studies are now showing that marital happiness is linked to fun? Specifically, *novel* experiences bring freshness and joy. Consider your courtship. Most likely you planned lively outings, created surprises, and even may have pushed daring boundaries a time or two for the sake of fun. For us the dating years were some of the best times in our lives—it was a fantastic adventure—and I even have scars to prove it! Let's learn from our former romantic selves and resuscitate fun in our marriage.

There is a Greek word for the "friendship" kind of love, *philos*, which means a trusted confidant; someone dearly loved in a personal, intimate way. Intimacy often results from rich time together. When a couple has this kind of a friendship, even ordinary tasks, like grocery shopping, can become fun outings. Think of the person you enjoy being with most on the planet. If it is your spouse, what a gift! If it is someone else, think about how you can act the same way in your marriage as you do with that person. Treat your spouse as your best friend, and fill up your fun bucket together.

GROW UP TOGETHER

The other day I got a text from a cousin who grew up with me in the same town, but who I don't get to see very often in our adult life. It read, "The older I get the more I miss you." And my heart ached, because I miss my cousin too. There is something about growing up with people—they see you through many awkward stages and as a result, really know you. Not that surface kind of knowing, but that deep *I know who you are*—where you've been—and where you are headed—kind of knowing. It's a gift that, with age, we both value more and more.

Marriages are like that. Embrace the awkward seasons as much as the vibrant ones. It is all a part of learning *to know*. Knowing takes time, and it requires the investment of minutes and years. Consider what you can do to encourage growth together.

My husband and I both are people of strong faith, but we mainly nurture our faith independently. Having a prayer time one morning a week before the kids rise converts that solitary pursuit to one that draws us closer together as a couple and to God. It has been a catalyst for transformation and renewal in countless ways in our relationship.

We also have a passion for the outdoors. Spending time in nature, seeking adventure, draws us close and creates common experiences that fills our relationship bucket.

Do you and your spouse both love music? Do you like to cook? Is serving others internationally a passion? Whatever it is, find areas you can share in together. Shared experience over a long period of time is a key ingredient for growing together rather than apart.

EVALUATE YOUR MARRIAGE REGULARLY

Sometimes I ignore the scale in my bathroom and push it into the corner. I pretend it isn't there because I don't want to know what it has to say. After days of seeing it peeking at me, I reluctantly step on. Sometimes I breathe a sigh of relief—not too bad. Other times my heart races and I have to fight chucking the machine out the door. No matter the results, it is a good thing for me to know my current weight because it indicates *where I need to go—how to proceed.*

Take the time you need, whether that is weekly, monthly, or yearly, to evaluate your marriage. If possible, do this together with your spouse. You could try evaluating yourself first, then each other, if you are comfortable with this level of honesty.

marriage check-up
SELF-EVALUATION

1. I expect my spouse to complete me and to make me happy:

   NEVER   VERY LITTLE   SOMETIMES   VERY OFTEN

   COMMENTS:

2. I make choices to love, even when I don't feel like it.

   NEVER   VERY LITTLE   SOMETIMES   VERY OFTEN

   COMMENTS:

3. I forgive easily and freely.

   NEVER   VERY LITTLE   SOMETIMES   VERY OFTEN

   COMMENTS:

4. I make time for sex with my spouse.

   NEVER   VERY LITTLE   SOMETIMES   VERY OFTEN

   COMMENTS:

5. My close circle supports my marriage.

   NEVER   VERY LITTLE   SOMETIMES   VERY OFTEN

   COMMENTS:

marriage check-up
SELF-EVALUATION

6. I show kindness in small ways daily.

NEVER   VERY LITTLE   SOMETIMES   VERY OFTEN

COMMENTS:

7. I create and make time for fun.

NEVER   VERY LITTLE   SOMETIMES   VERY OFTEN

COMMENTS:

8. I tend to believe the best about my spouse.

NEVER   VERY LITTLE   SOMETIMES   VERY OFTEN

COMMENTS:

9. I work on finding ways/activities to promote growth in our marriage.

NEVER   VERY LITTLE   SOMETIMES   VERY OFTEN

COMMENTS:

10. I speak positively to my spouse, demonstrating respect & consideration.

NEVER   VERY LITTLE   SOMETIMES   VERY OFTEN

COMMENTS:

So … what happens when the giant bucket is full? It overflows. The water that has been filling the container, drop by drop, comes cascading down onto you and those around you like a waterfall. For better or for worse, everyone stands, covered in the overflow. Is the water pure and refreshing? Or is it muddied—more like sludge than a clear mountain creek?

I don't pretend to have quick and easy answers to a subject as deep and wide as marriage. Life can be complicated and painful. But consider this truth: Every drop of water in the bucket counts. Every drop of water eventually reaches the roots. Cultivating a healthy marriage relationship will grow a strong root system for your whole family.

Feeling hopeless in your marriage? Focus on depositing just one drop of life-giving water. It has probably taken years to get to where you are—bad habits spilling over and creating negative, destructive patterns. Your marriage won't be miraculously healed overnight. Yet, as the life-giving drops of water multiply, over and over again, soon the entire bucket is full and your lifeless marriage can be rejuvenated. Something new will emerge. Never underestimate the power of the small. It is, in fact, the *small actions repeated consistently over time that create change and deep roots in your relationship.*

The next time you are at a water park, stand under the bucket. If you don't go to the water park very often, you can think about this bucket as you are in the shower with water pouring over you. Let the water rush over your head and remember that this waterfall is made of thousands of tiny drops. They may be insignificant alone, but together they create power, just as action upon action does in your marriage.

RECLAIMING MARRIAGE
dares

• Make a choice of love or offer a small act of kindness to your spouse, even when you don't feel like it.

• Practice forgiveness over a matter you've been hanging onto in your relationship by moving through those 3 steps listed in the chapter.

• Hit the sack (wink).

• Create fun in your relationship today – even if only for a minute (dance in the kitchen, tickle, laugh, play a game, etc.).

• Think through one activity you can adopt this week to grow together. If it requires pre-planning, put a date on the calendar and make arrangements.

Chapter 5

RECLAIMING CHILDHOOD

It is easier to build strong children than to repair broken men.
–Frederick Douglass

*There are only two lasting bequests we can hope
to give our children. One of these is roots, the other, wings.*
–Hodding Carter

Last winter, one of my friends, Sheri, was driving her kids to school when a car in the oncoming lane hit the vehicle in front of her. Swerving out of the way, Sheri avoided impact and pulled her car to the side of the road. She got out and checked in with the woman who had caused the accident. Catatonic, the woman walked with Sheri toward the vehicle she had hit. Without warning, the woman turned on her heels toward Sheri's car, grabbed the door handle, and got in.

Sheri tried desperately to get her out, while her children struggled, unsuccessfully, to free themselves from the vehicle. My friend watched in horror as the woman lurched the car into drive, and then drove away with her most precious cargo inside.

The horrible sensation of hijacking can hit our families. We watch, dumbfounded, as our children are taken by any number of things: bullying, pressures to conform, sports, perfectionism, mean-girl friendships, social media, video games, alcohol, pornography, drugs, sex, the list goes on. We can stand and watch as the negative forces threaten to drive off with our kids, or jump in and pull them out of danger. No one else will fight for our children like we will. We are the difference makers in the lives of our children.

Being a parent is the most vulnerable, difficult, and raw position I will ever fill. It is also a rich, soul-reaching, honored, blessed role—one that takes every fiber of my being in effort and care. It's the area I feel the most significant rewards and the deepest sorrows. Caring so deeply hurts—the kind of emotion that reaches down and squeezes my heart, until I feel crushed.

While I know full well the limits of my abilities as a mom, I also have come to know that a parent's love is a force that transcends fault, distance, time, and obstacles. It is strong. Bravely strong. It is a kind of love that pursues valiantly, even when ignored. It sits day after day at the counter tutoring in math after school. It forges countless circles of prayer around a teenager's room, and gets up with a baby after only two hours of sleep. It keeps growing, trying, and transforming, knowing that we can always be better for our kids. A parent's love fiercely protects—standing in the full face of the negative influences of culture saying, "Not here. You may surround us, but this territory belongs to me."

If I have learned anything in raising kids, it is that there is no formula to follow, even though we long for simplistic answers. Each family must discern, pray, and figure out how to best lead their crew through this life. However, there are some specific areas that have been hijacked, which we, as parents, can take back.

FEAR HIJACKS COURAGE

Parenting takes backbone. It is not for the timid. We must have the fortitude to stand up for what we know to be true and right. If you feel it's best to call parents to verify plans every single time your teen daughter goes out, do it, knowing there is plenty of trouble to be had by today's youth. If you need to go meet with the principal of your son's school due to a bullying issue and show up at lunch every day for a month, *go*. Your child's sense of safety is in your hands. If you need to put that three year old in time out for the twentieth time today, it's worth the effort. If you decide to put limits on the demanding sports schedule, take the resistance you will receive as a badge of courage.

Nelson Mandela once said, "Courage is not the absence of fear, but the triumph over it. The brave man is not one who does not feel afraid, but he who conquers that fear." There is hardly anything that plagues parents more than fear. There is so much unknown when it comes to parenting. We fear our kids will be physically or emotionally hurt; we fear that what we offer as parents will not suffice; and we fear that what we teach and model will not be enough to keep them on a virtuous path, away from the negative trappings of culture. Let's lean into that fear and as Mandela so beautifully says, triumph over it. No one else is going to take the steps needed to protect the hearts of our children. This falls on us. Take the challenge seriously and follow through with grit. The next time you are faced with feelings of fear, stop and acknowledge the emotion, then take a deep breath. Make a decision to respond with courage.

MEDIA HIJACKS INNOCENCE

Our children are the first generation of kids growing up with unlimited connectivity to multimedia devices. We are not even sure yet what the long-term effects will be and how it will impact their future, their relationships, and their health. We can, however, work with what we do know. While most of us agree that technology is extremely helpful and positive, we also know that violent video games, constant connection to social media, and too much screen time is not. Every family has to decide for themselves the right age to give their child an electronic device and when they are ready to experience the world of technology. Likewise, it is important to realize that though it may be easier at the moment for us to allow our kids to watch a movie, play a game, or check social media, it may not be the best long-term choice for them. When we parent with the long-term in mind, these decisions become easier to discern.

Hear this clearly: Parents, you are in control. You do not need to give in to the pressure that exists because everyone else has _____ (some electronic device) or gets to _____ (some questionable activity). Your child does not need to have constant access to media, or be allowed access to all of the media choices available. This is a message I remind myself of on a regular basis with my teen because sometimes I forget who is really in control of those choices.

I also encourage every home to have a strong filter on every device in the home—computers, tablets, phones, iPods, etc. Predators, pornography, and other pitfalls threaten to lure our children into their dangerous grip. The risk is simply too great to ignore. It is critical that we do not take an overwhelmed mindset toward media, but approach it offensively and come up with a plan. If you can't figure it out yourself, find someone who can help. What kids are exposed to in childhood and adolescence creates formative pathways in the brain. These engrained patterns will be very difficult to break as adults and will affect their future relationships, marriages, and homes.

We will not be able to control everything our kids are exposed to in regards to media. No matter how vigilant we are, inevitably something will sneak through the back door. Alongside these safeguards, we must educate our kids so they are equipped to handle situations when they occur. Because we are afraid to take their innocence from them, we may hesitate to teach about the darker side of the Internet and media. We must be discerning in this process, but it is better for your child to hear information from you, a trusted parent, rather than the kid who sits beside him in math class, or worse, to fall prey to an abusive situation online. Education on technology dangers also takes some of the curiosity and mystery away from sensitive subjects. Set aside special time to address issues like these—even if it is a bit awkward, especially in the beginning.

In our family we have multiple devices. My kids speak the language of technology. It is a common occurrence to have sometimes heated "discussions" about the use or privileges surrounding these items, especially with my oldest. Expect push back. You will get it. Your kids' friends may have few or no limits. That becomes the yardstick by which your kids will measure your rules. Make your decisions based on your own moral compass as a parent, not by what everyone else is doing.

Technology use is an area where kids might attempt to wear you down. If this is the case, or if your children work better with concrete guidelines, write down the agreed upon media expectations and post them somewhere visible. Then, when a guideline is violated, you can simply point to the chart rather than get in a power struggle. As kids grow older and as technology changes quickly, guidelines may be adapted. New freedoms are appropriate with maturity and communication.

Here are a few of our guidelines *as examples*. These may or may not be what you choose to implement, but they will get you thinking about your standards for media. These may evolve as our children grow, but for now, here are a few we implement:

- Check-in phones at night
- Browsers are turned off
- Parents have the passwords to all devices
- Parents can check any device at any time and are allowed to "spot check"
- Parents are "friends" or "followers" on social media and have access to all content
- Parents must approve all apps

We also have some general guidelines that shape how technology is used when we are with others. For example, we often ask that devices be put away when other people are present. As a parent, your children are watching whether or not you comply with these guidelines as well. If we want our children to abide by certain standards of behavior, we have to model those ourselves. Give your family permission to call you out if you are breaking the rules.

Every family must decide what is comfortable for them when it comes to these agreements, but keep in mind that it is much easier to allow more freedoms over time than to take them away after they've been given. Whatever you do, be consistent and make sure that everyone is aware of the rules. Clear boundaries help with a subject already complicated and difficult.

If you are in a situation where your child has already been exposed to some harmful material, whether pornography, violence, or other, the natural response is panic. Transform that panic into purpose. Resolve to open up communication, get any help your child needs, and educate yourself on how to protect your child from today forward. No guilt over what you *should* have done before. It's time to *get brave*, focus on the present and see it as an opportunity to grow and educate.

Questions to ask:

- Are computers in a public area of the home, rather than a private space?
- Are parental controls on? Is there a filtering system in place on every device? Including televisions?
- Do children have unlimited access to media, or is there a daily plan and rhythm to create more balance?
- What are the ratings of the video games children play?
- Is social media use monitored regularly?
- Is everyone in the family aware of the specific expectations related to devices and media?
- Are movie ratings monitored?
- What filters (if any) are on devices in friends' homes? Ask them. This is sensitive, but choose to be brave.

ACTIVITIES HIJACK FREE TIME

Tears filled my eyes as I rushed into cooking group, late. It seemed I was disappointing everyone. My kids had been late to practice because I physically could not get everyone where they needed to go by the time they needed to be there, and then I had let my own group down by arriving late. However, the tears signaled more than simple tardiness; they were a symptom of exhaustion. During high sports season, my family often runs on full throttle and it compromises the emotional health of us all.

Growing up, I was a competitive athlete who took my sports seriously, but it was a different environment for activities. Most of us remember our childhood involvements as healthy, balanced experiences that helped build us into who we are as people and still left time for unstructured play. Now, in order for children to be successful, there is pressure to start them in competition at younger and younger ages, run them all year long in the activity of choice, and compromise family time to make way for achievement. Even if this is a cultural norm, we can decide how we are going to approach this norm. There is not a right or wrong answer to this dilemma, but instead of blindly following the pattern set by others, let's think through our decisions.

Here are some questions that will help:

- At what age is it reasonable to start our children in competitive sports or activities? The answer may vary for different children within the same family.
- Is there a certain day of the week that we will not play sports or participate in other activities?
- What kinds of activities trump games/practices/meetings? How do we communicate to the coach or leader of the group about this?
- Is there a limit to the number of activities in which our children can participate at one time?

Last spring, we made a decision to keep one of our children out of a game on a Sunday due to a family event. The coach was not happy about our decision. Expect that. There will be times when others do not agree with your judgment, and that's okay. Our point of reference may not be the same as the norm. The important thing is that we respectfully communicate and live with integrity in our decisions. We don't skip a game just because we don't want to make the effort to show up; we make those decisions based on value judgments that have been carefully weighed.

A little creativity can help intermingle family time and activities. Some families choose to make game time, family time. Everyone goes and cheers on siblings. I have one friend who periodically sets up picnics during games. She makes the soccer field a fun family outing. When my kids are at piano lessons, I make it a point to talk to the one who is waiting for his turn. This is built in one-on-one time.

Some of our children will blossom into greatness in their activity of choice, but most will simply enjoy an activity and then move into adult life. Their experiences will help shape them, grow them, and teach them many important virtues, but they may not all be stars. Most will not stand on a podium and wear an Olympic medal, or receive a full ride scholarship to the Julliard School of Music. Does that make our children's involvements any less significant? Absolutely not, but let's keep fun in mind, and allow sports and activities to add to our lives and not run them.

NEGATIVITY HIJACKS A POSITIVE RELATIONAL CLIMATE

Every holiday I bring down a box from the garage to decorate our center island in the kitchen. In fall, pumpkins, leaves, and candles line the miniature antique ladder. At Christmas there are poinsettias and Snow Village houses. Valentine's Day? Hearts, mailboxes, and candy hearts. As the center of activity, it is the perfect place to create a festive mood in our house.

While my seasonal decorating creates a holiday mood, every day we are creating a relational atmosphere that influences the climate of our home. We set the scene with the words we use or don't use, the way we interact, and how we spend time. When we see our children, what is written on our faces? Do we communicate that we are delighted with their presence? Or frustrated? Do we speak in angry, harsh tones, or ones that build up and encourage? Are people allowed to put each other down through biting sarcasm? All of these elements whirl together to create the tenor of our home. I can easily become discouraged when I don't like what I am seeing—both in my kids and in myself. When I get to that point, I can either throw up my hands and give up, or make a decision to change the climate, starting *with me*.

Here are some ways to help create an uplifting tone:

• **Be glad to see them**:
One day I picked up my daughter from school, as usual. As she got in the car I muttered, "Hi." She said, "What's wrong?" I asked what she meant. "Normally you are so happy to see me. What's wrong?" This underscored an important ritual that I hadn't fully recognized. It matters how we greet our kids. When they get up, when they get home from school, when they come down the stairs, what is our response? My younger two boys often take the bus home. When they walk down the sidewalk, I make it a point to swing the door wide open and sing, "Welcome home boys!" One of them now says it even before I open the door. Think through what you are communicating by your greetings—it will shape how they feel about being at home.

• **Weigh words with care:**
Walking down the Northwood Junior High middle school hallway, a boy turned to me and spit out some harsh words that cut to the core. He felt left out of a group, and this was his way of getting revenge. There is very little I remember about seventh grade, but this scenario is forever burned in my mind. Each one of us can point to specific times in our lives when a person spoke words that were hopeful and helped us reclaim joy, or other times when someone spoke words that hijacked our hopes and we fell flat.

Words are powerful. What we say matters. As parents, the words we speak have even more weight because our kids' hearts are wide open to our influence due to our position in their lives. When we make hurtful comments, they cut deeply. Most of us know this, but sometimes the emotion of the moment leads to a reckless tongue. Because our affirmation and acceptance are so important for our children, this harshness shakes their foundation like an earthquake. Remaining calm and in control of our speech is one of the greatest gifts we can give our children. One of my favorite proverbs says, "Words kill, words give life; they're either poison or fruit—you choose." (Proverbs 18:21, MSG) So what will *you* choose? Your answer will profoundly impact your family.

Words that kill:

- Belittling
- Hurtful insults
- Comparisons
- No words—stonewalling or ignoring
- Frustrating or "fed up" tones

Words that bring life:

- Kind statements
- Encouragement
- Joyful speech
- Healing words—forgive me, I'm sorry
- "I believe in you" statements

PLACES OF PRESSURE HIJACK SAFE HAVENS

The school bus, playground, or locker room may be a place of pressure for your child. Whether they are subject to outright bullying, or just their own insecurities and feelings of inadequacy, some physical spaces feel unsafe for our children. There are few places in our culture where kids feel truly at home, away from criticism, insecurity, judgment, and strife. The stronger roots our children have in positive spaces, the better able they will be to navigate pressured situations.

Today I am writing from Camp Spalding, a retreat center one hour away from our home. We are finishing up a few days of a family camp full of zip-lining, water wars, hikes, talks by the campfire, and great food—both for our bodies and our souls. We've been coming here for years with several other families and our kids have grown up together. To our children, this camp is one of their safe places in the world. They get the chance to experience freedom in a secure environment, try new experiences, and bond with other families. This summer some of my daughter's friends went to their camp specifically for high school students. On the way home, their parents listened with tears in their eyes as their daughters recounted the freedom they felt to simply be themselves, and what it was like for them to feel deeply valued by those around them. There weren't any pressures to be someone other than who they were uniquely created to be—and this gave them wings. This camp has become a refuge—a place for kids of all ages to see themselves and God in new and fresh ways. They get to practice being themselves in a positive, healthy, natural environment, away from the distractions and the negative pressures of culture, and that translates to other areas of their lives. *Safe havens provide opportunity for roots of identity to grow.*

A sense of place is simply a significant connection to a geographic area—emotionally, physically, or spiritually. Research supports that childhood play in natural settings helps create a healthy sense of place. Creativity and a strong inner self are encouraged and grown when there is time to explore, create, and dream. There is a peace and calm in nature that settles over our souls like a warm blanket on a cold day. As parents we are often more apt to hand a restless child an electronic device rather than requiring him or her to go create their own play outside. While occasional electronic use is no big deal, as parents it is important to recognize this trend and to counter it with intentional experiences that promote growth and connection to the outdoors. As you look for safe places for your children, consider how you can couple those with an exposure to the outdoors. It will have double the impact.

Where can your children go to find safe havens? Whether the sanctuary is a local park, a campground, a grandparent's house, a recreation center, or a church youth group, make time in the schedule for your children to spend time there, even if it requires sacrifice.

POOR FRIENDSHIPS HIJACK STRONG CHARACTER

Friendships are one of life's joys. They bring laughter, understanding, acceptance, and community. We are all better when we spend time with friends—they expand our horizons beyond our families and add diversity to our lives. Sometimes, however, a friendship can become unhealthy, or even toxic. Like a leaky pen, the dark ink runs to areas we don't want, and leaves a messy stain. Those unhealthy friendships can have significant negative impact if we are not careful.

My sister once said to me, "I can't control who my children become friends with at school, but I can nurture certain friendships outside of school." She has made it a point to surround her family with positive influences outside of school hours, including cousins, who make great friends.

In friendship, whether as adults or children, we are often either pulling someone up, or being pulled down. A wise parent sees when their child is being pulled to a place of compromise or damage and intervenes.

Teach your children the following characteristics of good friends:

- Good friends allow you to be yourself without criticism.
- Good friends tell the truth, and don't try to hide things from you, or make you keep secrets.

- Good friends treat you with respect and don't put you down, in private or in public.
- Good friends give you space, and don't get jealous when you have other friendships.
- Good friends offer care, trust, kindness, forgiveness, and patience.
- Good friends support the person you are—with all of your unique gifts and talents. They don't try to pressure you to be anyone different or to conform to who they want you to be.
- Good friends are a treasure. When you find one, hang on!

Remember Sheri's kids who were hijacked? Through a series of dramatic and providential events, my brave friend, with the superhuman strength that lies in the lion's heart of a mother, seized an opportunity. The stolen car went about thirty yards before the driver rammed into the first car again. That allowed enough time for Sheri to catch up to her children who were trapped inside and yell instructions for them to get out. Sheri's oldest son, who sat in the front seat, punched the woman to try and stop her from driving. Her other son kicked the back door open, and moving swiftly, Sheri yanked out her daughter. The woman took off again, totaled the car, and ended up in the intensive care unit of the hospital. Sheri rescued her children—and so can you. The negative influences of culture are powerful, but as parents, we are stronger. Believe it and never, ever give up hope.

THE FRIENDSHIP test

Use this chart to help your child discern whether or not someone is a good friend to him/her.
Check True (T) or False (F)

My friend is trustworthy.	T	F
My friend tells me the truth and doesn't lie about little or big things.	T	F
My friend allows me to be myself and supports the person I am.	T	F
My friend doesn't try to pressure me to do things I don't want to do.	T	F
My friend builds me up and doesn't talk about me behind my back.	T	F
My friend allows me to have other friendships without getting jealous.	T	F
My friend forgives me, even when I make mistakes.	T	F
My friend is there to help me when I need it, or when I am sad.	T	F
My friend makes my life better.	T	F

RECLAIMING CHILDHOOD
dares

• Implement a media change in your home. Whether that is checking in phones during dinner, placing a filter on computers and devices, or limiting video game time, take a brave step in regards to media.

• Spend 5 minutes of concentrated, fully engaged time with each of your children today.

• Put a date on the calendar to spend one on one time with one of your children.

• Get outside with your kids. Take a hike, go to a park, or dig in the backyard.

• Tell each child something you specifically notice about him or her that is encouraging and positive.

Chapter 6

RECLAIMING PLAY

There is little success where there is little laughter.
–Andrew Carnegie

We don't stop playing because we grow old,
we grow old because we stop playing.
–George Bernard Shaw

W arm conversation and a group of women circled the blazing bonfire. Sparks popped and landed as if on parade as we sung happy birthday to our friend, Melanie. We live up north, and there are only a couple months out of the year when the nights are warm and balmy. We relished the clear night sky and the humming of the cricket chorus as the waves lapped up on the shore. "These are the nights for skinny dipping." I blurted out, sure that the others would agree. "Skinny dipping? What?" several asked surprised. "Wait ... you've gone, right?" I asked. Their faces told me the answer. They had never been! Growing up in lake country, it was a rite of passage ... one that my friends needed to experience.

Marching out to the dock along with the other skinny dipping veterans, we flung off our clothes into the darkness and dove in. The others stood on the dock, nervously laughing and shaking their heads. "YOLO!" we yelled from the water (you only live once). After minutes of pleading, finally everyone jumped in, even the greatest resister. We are sure we woke up all of the neighbors with our screams and laughter. That night imprinted a memory because we did something out of the ordinary.

Sharing fun experiences bonds people. Hearts are sewn together by an invisible thread when we laugh and enjoy life alongside each other. This is why companies pay large amounts of money to take their staff on team building adventures, such as a daylong ropes course. They know that the time spent doing something creative, where people can work together, laugh, and share experiences will pay large dividends in their workplace community. If it is valuable to laugh and play with our friends and coworkers to build better relationships, it is even more so within our families. We want to create the closest, most loving, tight-knit community as possible at home, and an essential secret ingredient in that recipe is fun and play.

My daughter informed me the other day that children laugh 300 times a day, and adults only fifteen. While I have not been able to substantiate this fact, it is easy to observe that as we get older, we do indeed laugh less. Perhaps it is because there are more pressures, disappointments, and difficulties. Life can be very hard. But perhaps it is also because, somewhere along the way, we became very serious ... too serious. Some of us have become downright grumpy. We have forgotten how to laugh and play, a response once so natural in childhood.

A poignant proverb says, "A cheerful disposition is good for your health; gloom and doom leave you bone tired." (Proverbs 17:22, MSG) Recent research has proven this statement, finding that laughter is physically good for us, stimulating blood flow, boosting our mood, and decreasing blood pressure and stress hormones. Beyond personal benefits, however, laughter also creates strong bonds with others by fostering a strong sense of intimacy.

Most people tend to be one of two types: work before play, or play before work. As parents, it's hard not to be work, work, work, work. There are endless tasks and our jobs are never really done. Whether you are a stay-at-home or working parent, the challenge remains the same: *Stop*. We can go through an entire day doing many good things *for* our families, but not really connecting *with* them. While the tasks are important, they are not more important than relationships.

My sister, Kendra, is a ten on the fun scale. She is one of those people who knows how to work hard, but then also determines when it's time to stop and enjoy life and the people around her. When Kendra shows up, life is more joyful and lighthearted. You, too, can embrace these qualities in your home. Work hard, but then put work aside when it's time to connect, joke, giggle, *and lighten up*. Every day. If needed, put specific boundaries on your work hours. For example, you may decide that no work is allowed after 7 p.m., or that playtime begins at 6 p.m. Whatever is needed to ensure follow through, make it a habit to stop and enjoy one another. To children, T-I-M-E spells love, and one of their favorite ways to spend time is to play. Think through how to incorporate play and fun into your family's daily rhythm.

PLAY LIKE A KID

Even if you only can play for a few minutes each day with your child, that investment fuels relationship. Get on the ground and build a Lego Star Wars character, rock the baby doll and change her diaper, or jump on the trampoline. If you have teens, play their favorite sport in the yard with them before practice, listen to one of their favorite songs sharing ear buds, laugh over funny YouTube videos, or arm wrestle. Reach back in your bank of memories and remember how you loved to spend time as a young person. Be a student of your children and watch what gets them excited. Allow them to direct play activities and follow their lead. As parents there are many rules and boundaries that we put on our children. Play is one of those areas we can relax and allow them the freedom to explore and experiment without limitations.

Our crew loves backyard kickball. Whenever my kids come running in to tell me they are playing, I drop whatever I'm doing and head outside. It's a fun, easy way to connect with them and get some exercise as a family at the same time.

DO THE UNEXPECTED

Today at our family's lake cabin it began to rain hard, pounding the water in thick, heavy droplets. In a moment of spontaneity, we put on our swimsuits, ran down the dock, and jumped in the lake. Swimming is fun, but swimming while it's pouring rain is *really* fun. My daughter, McKenna, couldn't find her suit, and not wanting to miss out, leaped in with clothes on. There is something about doing regular activities in a fresh or unexpected way that makes them memorable and exciting.

Think through your regular routine and consider how you can introduce a surprise element into a set activity. Get everyone in their pajamas and ready for bed, then call them out to the front porch for cookies and milk while you read a bedtime story. Drive the same route to school, but stop and have a five-minute donut date. Carpool to soccer, but instead of taking everyone home as usual, stop to let them jump in the town river or fountain. Last spring I went to have lunch with my son at the elementary school cafeteria. On the way I stopped at the store and grabbed two bags of value-pack Popsicles. When I sat down next to Hudson and his friends, I pulled out the surprise. Delighted, Hudson ran around the lunchroom handing out the treats. It was the simplest act, but I still have kids talking to me about the day I brought Popsicles to school.

GET THE FAMILY OUTSIDE

There was a time when my husband and I were struggling with secondary infertility. During this painful season of life, I went snowshoeing high in the Selkirk Mountains of Idaho. As I steadily climbed, I broke through a dense, thick layer of fog. Bright sunlight and blue skies welcomed me on the other side. As I looked at jagged peaks that stretched into Canada, with the thick blanket of fog below, I visually saw my problem. While I walked around blindly in the fog, God saw clearly above it. My future was not a mystery, but was clearly known. Whether I ever became pregnant again or not, I did not need to fear. Above the fog was clarity, I just couldn't always see it. The comfort I received that day in nature healed a part of me that had been very wounded.

Time spent in nature has a way of reaching to the soul of a person, whether it is an adult or a child. It calms a troubled spirit, rejuvenates a broken heart, and fills us with hope. It quiets us so that we can listen and hear. In a world filled with fast-paced technology, nature is a welcome respite. Spending time in nature births the creativity and wonder that makes life interesting. Whether our kids recognize it or not, they need this influence, emotionally and physically. I also find that nature breathes enough space to have great conversations. We are more in touch with ourselves and with others when we clear away distractions.

Whether you live in the city or the country, find some outdoor spaces that are easy for your family to access on a regular basis. Perhaps your child will discover a favorite tree on your block, or plant a pot full of vegetables on the patio and watch them grow. Getting outside in the fresh air and noticing the world around you is refreshing. If you live in an area abundant with natural resources, take advantage of them. Climb mountain trails, paddle rivers, and skip rocks.

Watch children interact with nature. Sticks become swords, fire starters, spears, or art tools. Rocks are treasures. Sand is formed into castles. Flowers, leaves and pinecones become décor. Snow offers opportunities for cave building and sledding. Nature provides the playground—we simply need to step outside.

Here are some ideas to help you get outside into nature:

- Go on a walk and jump in puddles
- Lay on the ground and watch the clouds or stars
- Play hopscotch or four-square using chalk
- Take a hike and learn about animal tracks
- Camp out—even if it is only in the back yard
- Skip rocks
- Play capture the flag
- Take a bike ride to a favorite spot
- Have a snowball fight
- Plant a garden or an herb pot
- Create obstacle courses
- Build a fort
- Take a moonlight or sunrise hike
- Gather outdoor materials and create a craft or animal home
- Berry pick at a local farm
- Fish at a local pond or river
- Swim or canoe in a lake in the morning or by moonlight
- Snowshoe or ski
- Build a campfire
- Collect interesting rocks

INTEGRATE MUSIC

Music is a party staple. Why? Because music is a catalyst for fun. Everyone loves grooving to classic tunes, or keeping a beat to new ones. One of my favorite things in the whole world is when McKenna plays the piano while I'm cooking dinner. It fills the house and creates a warm, cozy mood. When our kids wash dishes at night, Michael Jackson can often be found blasting from the speakers. Michael can even make washing dishes fun!

Music can also help those in the family who are struggling with feelings of loneliness or depression. It has a mood-boosting component that lifts the spirit, and provides comfort. If you notice someone struggling in your family, or if you are experiencing those feelings yourself, select positive and upbeat music for your home.

Consider how you can create a festive mood by incorporating music. Whether you put it on while you work as a family, enjoy a concert in the park, or have a spontaneous family dance party on the deck, use music to foster play and fun.

MAKE MESSES

The reality of creative play is that it often creates a mess. Forts use every blanket in the house, watercolor painting requires a space to dip and brush, and cutting snowflakes out of paper leaves little white scraps all over the floor. While we like the idea of play, the reality is that we often don't do an activity because of the potential mess. My son, Stetson, is a lemonade stand shark. He would run his lucrative home business every day of the summer if I'd let him. But every time he asks me if he can do a stand, I picture sticky lemonade spilling all over the floor, splashing drops all the way to the door. It makes me want to say, "No." Yet, I know in my mothering core that a little inconvenience for me is worth the experience for him. I don't have to let him do it every day, but I'm learning to say, "Yes" as often as I can. There are many things I have to say, "No" to as I raise my tribe, especially as they get older, and I've decided a lemonade stand is not one of them.

Designating a space in the home for creative play is a way to encourage artistic expression, and also contain the mess. I have a friend who keeps tubs full of sand and various Tonka diggers. Her preschooler opens the lid and plays, keeping the sand and the tractors inside of the tub. When he's done, he puts the lid back on and puts the sand away. Another friend has a craft area on a counter. She keeps stickers, glitter, glue, scissors, and paper all within reach. Keeping it contained to one area of the house helps her, and yet her children always have the option to go create their masterpieces in a space that is designated for messes.

Let's be honest. Our desire for a clean house often trumps our desire for our kids to explore and create. Ultimately we must deal with that truth and decide what is, long-term, more important. We have to mentally give our children and ourselves permission to make a mess, then let go of the need to control. It's good for all of us. Part of learning to play again is learning how to embrace a bit of messy living.

SPEND ONE-ON-ONE TIME

"Dad, thanks again for taking me climbing." Our son, Dawson, said for the tenth time that day. He and Erik had just summited Mt. Adams, a tall peak in Washington State. Gratitude and confidence exuded from his sunburned face. It was a difficult trek, but he did it very well. My husband told me later that nothing could replace the look on his face as he stood on the top and gazed at the world from the summit. That experience bonded them deeply. One-on-one time with kids does that. It allows us to focus on what is meaningful and fun for that particular child, and tailor our time together accordingly. Dawson thrives in the outdoors. With this knowledge, Erik planned a trip that would be relationship-building for them, but also would light passion in our son.

To some kids, climbing a mountain would not be their idea of a good time, but to Dawson, it was a home run.

In the midst of everyday life we can forget how significant it is to spend time alone with each of our children and play with them. My daughter and I go on a special weekend every year. The purpose of this time is twofold: to talk about issues or challenges she is facing at that stage of life, and to have fun and simply enjoy each other's company. Without fail, I walk away from that weekend amazed at how connected we feel. Why do I forget the impact of these set apart times in the midst of routine?

Whether you have only one child, or multiple, spending individual time with our kids communicates, "I love you enough to single you out, carve out the space, and focus my energies on *just you*." That is powerful. It means more than all of the best intentions in the world, because it sends a message of priority. Kids need to know that they matter, that someone is *for them* in this life. It's hard to think of a better way to communicate that than one-on-one time. And it isn't always easy to carve out time to be focused on one child, especially in a bigger family.

In large families, especially, think in terms of one-on-one *moments*. When you are driving one of your children to soccer practice, for example, exercise that mindset and make the most of your time with that child. Put on her favorite music, be interested in her hobbies and friends, and give her a favorite snack. If you are making dinner, and one of your kids is in the kitchen, stop and hug him. Ask him if he'll sample some of the food for dinner that night, and surprise him with a small treat. Grab hold of little moments to deepen roots with each child.

Even if a child is at first reluctant to connect, persevere. It's your best chance to melt an icy exterior. Personally, I would say that carving out one-on-one time has had more positive impact on our relationships than anything else we've done in parenting.

One of my friends has a child whom she considers "the easy one." Her daughter seemed to enter the world with a smile on her face. A natural peacemaker, she works to create harmony in the home and in the family relationships. Because she is so low maintenance, my friend often feels that she spends significantly more time with the other kids who require more focus, discipline, and monitoring. In short, she feels that she ignores the easy one, therefore unintentionally punishing her for being so great. One-on-one time helps with this dynamic too. Children, who may not naturally get as much focus for any reason, thrive and blossom with the attention.

Study your children as individuals and consider how you can use one-on-one time to have fun and play with each of them. I guarantee the time will be a smashing success if you begin with your child in mind as you plan.

Ideas for One-on-One Moments:

- *Have a time each night or each week dedicated to one-on-one time.*

   Each day pick a different person who gets that special slot. If you have a preschooler, choose simple activities. Pick up crayons and color for a few minutes together, asking her what colors you should use, or play hide and seek.

- *Plan dates.*

   Take kids out to ice cream, to the park, or to a coffee shop. Make the time special and give your full attention.

   Once a year take a weekend trip

   Once a year, take a child on an entire weekend. Make the time intentional. Have fun, but also be prepared to talk about important issues going on in his/her life. When I prepare for our special weekend, I do some research on the topic we are going to cover. This becomes a great springboard for discussion.

It's fine if we don't cover all of the material, but bringing helpful information into our weekend facilitates conversations.

- *Coming of age traditions*
  When kids reach certain ages, plan a unique way to celebrate it. For example, one friend takes her sixteen year old out to dinner with family and friends. The guests bring letters for the teenager and share wisdom on how to survive the teen years. There is more on these kinds of rituals in the traditions chapter.

- *Confidence builders*
  Set aside a day to teach your child a skill or nurture an interest. For example, my daughter has shown an interest in photography, so for Christmas I gave her a couple of lessons that we attended together. This was not only a fun time for her to learn, but it was also a great way to spend time together.

- *Go to camp*
  There are some fabulous organizations that specialize in parent-child experiences. Find a camp that has parent-child weekends, or that offers day activities or adventures. If you go to a family camp, set aside time with each child during that window.

Some of these ideas are simple, some are more involved. Do what you can. The essential idea is to participate in play with one child at a time on a regular basis, and deepen the roots of belonging through fun.

A Parent's
ONE-ON-ONE
Planning Guide

Name:

What does my child love to do?

What does my child get excited about?

What does my child like to talk about?

How could I help nurture a passion he/she has?

What means a lot to my child?

Where could we go that would be fun?

What activities could we do?

Plan:

A Child's ONE-ON-ONE Planning Guide

Name:

Write two activities you love doing:

1.

2.

Write two places you love going:

1.

2.

Write two of your favorite things:

1.

2.

Write two things you're passionate about:

1.

2.

RECLAIMING PLAY
dares

• Spend 5 minutes playing a favorite game with one of your children.

• Do a regular activity with an unexpected twist with your family.

• Put on the calendar a time to spend one on one time with one of your children.

• Whether it's snowy, sunny, or rainy, get outside with your family. Take a hike, go to a park, or dig in the backyard.

• Put on your favorite tunes and have a family dance party after dinner.

Chapter 7

RECLAIMING IMPERFECTION

I will hold myself to a standard of grace, not perfection.
–Emily Ley

You're imperfect, and you're wired for struggle,
but you are worthy of love and belonging.
–Brené Brown

O n a shadowy, autumn evening in the mountains, I came face-to-face with a black bear *inside* my parked car. I walked outside and saw the driver's side back door open. Thinking one of my kids left the door ajar, I shut it, not even bothering to look in the back. As I climbed in the driver's seat and turned the key, a low growl behind my right ear sent shivers up my spine. Terrified, I turned my head and found myself nose-to-nose with the intruder. Without thinking, I jumped out, slammed the driver's door and in doing so, locked the bear inside. The last thing I expected in my vehicle that night was a bear and it caught me completely by surprise.

Many parents today find themselves in a similar state: distraught and surprised. They climb into the vehicle of parenthood and discover something foreign. Overwhelmed by the responsibilities of parenting, and underwhelmed by the culture in which they parent, their experiences as parents don't look like what they expected. Days are frazzled with over-scheduled kids, too many tasks to accomplish, and not enough sleep. What happened to spontaneous backyard football games and laughing over a joke rather than arguing over curfew? Why are kids so disconnected from their families, but so connected to their electronic devices? Mothers and fathers wonder where they've gone wrong, and why they feel so fragmented. They are surprised that parenthood is so much harder than they expected.

There is a tension inherent to the human life that lends itself to constant discontent. We struggle with the gap between what we imagined life would be, what we desperately hoped or hope for, and what actually is our *present reality*. Whether these ideals are a result of ideas from our families of origin, or simply individual desires, we are often disappointed and disillusioned by the wide chasm. The ideal hangs in front of us, ever elusive. This is especially true when it comes to our families. Parenting and marriage are roles that, willingly or not, will torch perfectionism and idealism. These positions humble time and time again.

Whether it is a child who is not what a parent had hoped, a marriage that is strained, or a general feeling of discontent, most have or will struggle with the imperfect of life. While we enjoy and embrace the imperfection of a homemade cookie or a handcrafted card made by little hands, we do not share the same enthusiasm for the imperfect in our homes, our relationships, and ourselves. This prevents us from truly enjoying and appreciating our present reality. At some point we have to let go of what we thought life should be, and embrace what life *is*. That is, after all, where we live. I wonder what would happen if we leaned into the tension from which we are running? What if we embraced imperfect living as the very source of growth, change, and even joy, in our lives?

Sir Alexander Fleming, a scientist in the early 1900s, was searching for a wonder drug that could cure diseases. He threw away the experiments, as they were not producing the result he desired. One day Fleming noticed mold on a petri dish that he had discarded. It seemed to be dissolving all of the bacteria around it. When he grew the mold in the lab by itself, penicillin was born. What began as a failure turned into a powerful and lifesaving discovery.

While most of us are not in medical laboratories, we can see our role in the home in a similar light. What we see as imperfection or failure may very well be the source from which unexpected, deep beauty springs forth.

We have dear friends who had a baby several years ago. Nora was the long awaited girl in the family, following two older brothers. In the hospital, Kelly and Jim noticed that something about Nora didn't seem completely normal. After multiple tests, it was confirmed that Nora has Down syndrome. Reeling from the news, they delved into all of the emotion and logistics that information evokes in parents. Kelly describes feeling as if her baby had died. What she had imagined life would be with her child had just been shattered like a piece of fallen glass. She found herself holding those broken shards, desperately wondering how they would ever be put back together. Four years later, they marvel as life with Nora creates a mosaic more beautiful than they could have ever imagined. Nora is a pure soul. Not confined by social boundaries and rules, she is freed up to simply love people and the world with abandon. She brings a light into the room that disarms people. They shed insecurities and walls of protection around her. Nora truly *sees* people, and is in tune with their feelings in a way that her parents can't fully explain. It is because of Nora's Down syndrome that people let her into their world and their space in a way that is altogether astounding.

Kelly and Jim's family is different because of Nora. Their boys have a heightened awareness of anyone with special needs, and respond with compassion. They protect those who can't protect themselves, a sensitivity and awareness not often found in boys so young. They all have grown because of their surprise gift. Like Kelly and Jim's family, we can choose to embrace the imperfection of an unexpected situation, and see the potential for the new, profound beauty that it holds.

Striving for some made-up idea of perfection is exhausting, and one of the great deceptions we believe. It's a lie that there is even such a thing. All of life is a combination of joys, struggles, tears, laughter, pain, and passion, and many of these exist simultaneously. In fact, they enhance one another. We walk through mountains *and* valleys. Because of the valleys, we appreciate and absorb the mountaintop experiences differently. The valleys make us stronger, wiser, and offer perspective. The mountaintops offer rest, encouragement, peace, and joy.

My daughter's eighth grade year was one of my hardest parenting years to date. She suffered a seizure and severe concussion after fainting and falling head first off of the back of the choir bleachers on a very hot September day. Two more times she re-concussed during soccer games after being cleared to play. Her brain was fragile and not healing. Because it is difficult to discern whether or not the brain is healed after a concussion, we were walking a constant tightrope of fear and wisdom. We did not want to let her return to activities because we were afraid, yet to parent out of fear and not allow her the freedom to do what she loved was stifling. It was agonizing. To make matters worse, she was in *eighth grade*—a year when girls' emotions are not very steady. I couldn't tell what feelings and symptoms were because of the concussions, and what was just a product of being a young teen. That was a yearlong trek through a valley, for both of us. Though a bit worn, we are different because of our time spent there. Looking back at that very imperfect year, I see now that it deepened my compassion, built my faith, honed patience, and made me a stronger parent. I would not have asked for that, but am thankful for the way it changed me.

Whether you are in an imperfect situation by choice, or because of circumstances out of your control, what you *do* get to control is how you respond to challenges as they arise. It is often because of the shadow that we can see the light clearly. Let's stop running from the imperfect and uncomfortable, and instead lean into them—soaking up all of the depth, lessons, changes, and sincerity that those offer. It is here that we learn the rhythms of grace and deep love.

While reclaiming joy of the imperfect life is a lifelong process, there are a few guiding principles that will help us on our journey:

ACKNOWLEDGE YOUR OWN IMPERFECTION

I am chief among imperfect people and I live with others who are also just as flawed. There is hardly a day that goes by that we don't rub up against each other in some way or another. It's not easy, but it *is* good. Here we learn how to accept one another and work through difficulties in relationships.

I heard a speaker talk about a saying they have in their house, "everybody spills." They mean it literally as milk splashes over the table for the fifth time that week, but they also mean it figuratively. Because we are not perfect people, we will spill on other people as we go through life. Part of embracing the real is accepting that we, ourselves, spill. Are we authentic about that? Do we try to pretend that we don't have faults or make mistakes, or do we acknowledge them and do something about it?

The space between who we are on the inside and who we are on the outside is the degree of our authenticity. For example, do the people who are living in our home with us see the same person who shows up for Sunday church or for dinner with friends? Do we share authentically with people who have earned our trust, without pretense or hiding? Do we look at the *real* reasons we have certain behaviors and actions? Not the reasons we've made up in our heads to justify our behavior, but the true source of our motivations?

Living authentically means we live transparently and admit both failures and victories. We trade pretense for truth telling. When we mess up as parents, we go to our kids and tell them that. When we are having a hard day, we let our husband into the hurt places. It does not mean that we over-share with people we barely know, or expose the inner workings of our family to others when it would dishonor a family member to do so. Wisdom must accompany our authenticity. But as a concept internalized, when we embrace truth, we are better able to accept the good *and* the bad in our lives. It becomes a part of what is real and it makes us stronger. *Everybody spills!*

BURN THE YARDSTICK

Nothing will put a family or a person in an emotional coffin faster than comparisons. It puts to death what is good in our families and creates victims of "never enough."

I'm not sure I've ever struggled more in comparisons than in the young parenting years. It seemed that I always fell short of measuring up to what other moms were doing and how their kids seemed to be behaving so much better than mine. I wanted to be a good mom so badly, and this caused me to compare myself against how I was doing compared to everyone else. My kids are older now, and though we are all just as imperfect, I've come to realize that accepting all of us, as we are, is far superior to the made-up ideal. In fact, it is the variety and imperfections that have become most endearing over the years because those are the very things that make up *us*. We are a motley tribe, but it's our tribe, and we love it.

Comparisons breed a damaging self-focus. We are constantly assessing how something either reflects poorly or favorably on us. Either way, we lose. If we think we are better than someone, we fall into the trap of judgment. If we are less than, we succumb to jealousy. Both destroy relationships.

As parents, if we are constantly comparing our kids to others, they will feel that they are never enough. Our older kids already have to fight that everyday as they walk school hallways and sift through social media. They are comparing themselves to their peers all day long. They don't need us to be adding to that harmful burden. When we stop looking outward, comparing our parenting, our kids, and our family to others, we begin appreciating what is right in front of us.

One of the main sources of comparison is our feeling of inadequacy. When we don't feel confident in who we are, what we have, or in our skill set in an area, we begin to measure. This is when embracing imperfection helps significantly. If we come to peace with our own imperfections, whether personal or circumstantial, then we are freed up to love others instead of being threatened by them. When we are comfortable in our own skin, secure and confident, we can appreciate others in a way that is sincere and kind. This is also one of the greatest gifts we can give our children, as it models a strong sense of self that they can emulate.

The two best practices I have learned when fighting comparison are prayer and gratitude. I can pray for, or praise, the person or family with whom I am comparing. Practicing gratitude takes my eyes off others and focuses on the blessing of my situation. Developing these practices into habits in the form of a journal, words of affirmation, or prayers, lifts me out of comparison.

DON'T SWEAT THE SMALL STUFF

As a mom of a teenager, I laugh at how worked up I became over my first-born's grocery store tantrums, potty training, and whether or not she would share a toy. In the moment, those seemed monumental. Caring about those things was important, but if I could go back, I would change how I approached them. My perspective has changed.

Part of letting go of small stuff is embracing shortcomings and seeing the bigger picture. We relinquish controlling tendencies and allow others the freedom to practice life imperfectly. Ask yourself, "Is this going to matter one week, one month, or one year from now?" The answer to this question will help you discern whether something is big or small. Pausing before reacting to others in the family also helps in measuring our responses. Continuously worrying, nit-picking, or reprimanding our children will rob our homes of joy and shackle us to unhealthy emotions.

Though we don't like to admit it, sweating the small stuff is often a result of our tendency toward perfectionism. We want things to be a certain way, and when they are not, we break. One of my hot buttons is the cleanliness of the home. I like an orderly house. When my kids track in mud from their cleats, throw homework papers like confetti, and leave out their belongings, I come unglued. Yes, I want them to be responsible and clean up after themselves, but mostly, I just want a clean house. For me, chaos in the home creates chaos internally. I remember this when I'm about to yell at my kids about the disaster area. I still have them clean it up, but I change my approach, and don't get so wrapped up in every little detail. I try to choose to let the gratitude of having four amazing children, who are sometimes messy, wash away perfectionism.

If you are like me, then you read this section and cringed. I know that I often do not live with the bigger picture in mind. But give yourself the same grace we are advocating extending to others. Choose today to not sweat the small stuff, and let that be enough.

BE A GREAT FORGIVER

My husband is an amazing forgiver. He keeps short accounts and rarely remembers situations where I offend. That is the true definition of forgiver—someone who stops being angry or resentful of a person because of a mistake. This is a vital part of a healthy family. The reality is that we are going to make each other mad—often. That is what happens when flawed people live in close proximity.

Forgiveness requires a heart of humility. When we forgive, whether asked for or not, we choose to extend grace to others and willingly let go of the debt owed to us. It's a powerful action and it prevents anger, bitterness, and resentment from building a corrosive wall around our hearts.

In our family, we have made a distinction between "I'm sorry" and "Will you forgive me?" Sorry is for mistakes, or those things that hurt another person unintentionally. Asking someone for forgiveness is much harder because it acknowledges that something was done to hurt *on purpose*. It also gives the offended person a choice as to whether or not she'll let go of the offense by offering, "I forgive you." This is an important distinction, as forgiveness requires a heart of reconciliation from both. When we become a family of great forgivers, there is unity and peace.

SET OTHERS FREE

This year I planted three zucchini plants in my garden. One is growing gigantic leaves and thriving. The next one is medium sized, healthy but not flourishing. The third is barely any bigger than when it was planted. It doesn't seem to be growing as fast, or to be as rooted as the others. All of the plants came from the same nursery and were planted on the same day. Yet, all three are reacting differently to their environment and soil. The same is true for our kids. Each one will grow and develop at his/her own rate.

It is natural to want our kids to do great things, or to reach a certain place in their lives emotionally, physically, or spiritually. However, we must push aside expectations to make room for acceptance and growth. This has been a hard battle I've personally fought in parenting, as I tend toward idealism. When I've let go of my hopes or expectations, and have embraced individuality, peace follows. Our kids must blaze their own trails, at their own pace, not simply walk the ones we've traveled. It is vital that we communicate how much we love them where they are at, and often, *in spite of* their current state. That's love in action, and it creates powerful roots in the relational atmosphere of a home.

Identity is a central issue when we look at why we place expectations on our children. Enmeshment is a broad counseling term that means there is an unhealthy codependence in a relationship. It is when one person allows another person to define him or her. As parents, it is natural for us to want our kids to be successful, and to love what we love, thereby placing certain expectations on them. But what happens when they don't? What happens when our child inevitably disappoints? It's important to allow our children to be separate from us. What they do or don't do doesn't define who we are or shape our identity. When we have this perspective, we are better able to let go of unhealthy expectations that set others up for failure.

Most people, including our children, will not measure up to some aspect of how things "should" be. On the other hand, when someone does something kind unexpectedly, there is deep gratitude. Expectations and gratitude are opposite sides of a coin.

RECOGNIZE THAT LIFE IS NOW

We are living the fullness of our lives *right now*. Yesterday will not return, and tomorrow has not yet come. This present is all we have. Do we stop to look into the eyes of our child and appreciate that there is no one else on the planet like her? Do we appreciate the extended family dinner during a busy week, knowing that those people will not always be around? Do we cheer louder than anyone else on the sidelines for our child who just scored her first goal or for our child who is running hard, even if she may never score a goal?

Living with a perspective of the value of the present moment helps us let go of perfection. We simply breathe in the beauty of what is before us.

I don't pretend that there aren't frustrating moments. When my kids are arguing over who has to fold the laundry, instead of having a helpful spirit, I get frustrated. The "now" moment is not one that I want. However, I get to choose whether or not I will lean into the tension, frustrated that my kids are fighting, but thankful to have children and a washer and dryer that cleans our clothes for us.

Because we are flawed, we don't ever "arrive." This is a vital concept in accepting the journey of imperfection. There will never be a time when we feel we've got it all figured out. A part of our pilgrimage lies in coming to peace with the real and the unexpected, like the bear in the car. And also in realizing that we can have joy in our family, even in the midst of the crazy imperfections of our lives.

RECLAIMING IMPERFECTION
·dares·

• Share authentically with a close friend about how you are "really" doing or about a difficult circumstance you are facing.

• Speak kind words or encouragement to someone to whom you seem to consistently compare yourself.

• Identify one area of "small stuff" you've been sweating and shouldn't. Decide how to control your reaction triggers.

• What is one specific way you can allow _____ (insert name) to grow at his/her own pace?

• Let go of whatever expectations you are carrying toward _____ (insert name or situation). Make it a point to express gratitude instead.

Chapter 8

RECLAIMING
THE TABLE

The sun looks down on nothing half so good
as a household laughing together over a meal.
–C. S. Lewis

All great change in America begins at the dinner table.
–President Ronald Reagan

F
lickers of candlelight glowed on the cave walls as the only source
of light. The weathered farm table sat fifteen. Though most of
us did not share nationality, we did share one thing: a love for
genuine Swiss fondue. The restaurant tucked in the high mountain Alps
was the perfect backdrop for my 21ˢᵗ birthday. International chatter
accompanied the wine, garlic, and cheese rolled over thick, crusty pieces
of artisan bread. As the pot bubbled hot, so my soul settled into one of

the most memorable nights of my life. My study-abroad friends and I shared so much more than fondue that night—we feasted together at life's table—slowly sipping the white wine that was chosen to complement the fondue. We spoke of politics, culture, sports, and spirituality as we stretched cheese and soaked bread.

Fast-forward four years to another worn table on the other side of the world. A pig's large eyes stared at me. Costa Rica brought an education in both language and cuisine. Paulina, a frail grandmother with waist-length white hair, whipped the pig's head around and laughed as I winced at the sight. "I will teach you," she chided in Spanish and began to prepare the animal for the evening meal. Whether it was making homemade tortillas, beans with rice, or frying plantain, we shared cutting boards and tied heartstrings. The table offered us a common language, even though for many months I did not speak Spanish. Time around the table rescued me from the feelings of loneliness, isolation, and homesickness in this foreign land of toucans and coffee beans.

Spanning all cultures and socio-economic classes, the table is fellowship. It is a time when people stop in the midst of full lives and busy schedules to gather. We are doing so much more than breaking bread when we share a meal. We eat for sustenance, but it is more than just physical. It taps into the emotional connection between us as we clasp hands to pray, pass plates, and take in the smells and the feeling of "home." There is a mysterious transformation that occurs when people sit to enjoy a meal together—one that can't be fully defined, but only felt with the heart. I am certain that the space around the table is some of the holiest ground I ever tread. It is one of the main places where family is built. Hour upon hour, day after day, whether dining on the simplest soup or feasting like a king, the gathering, sharing, talking, laughing, arguing, and debating, weaves a tight bond that shapes who we are and who we become, both as people, and as a family.

In other countries, people often plan their days around cooking and the family meal. We have a friend from France who says, "The food does not wait for us, we wait for the food!" In contrast, the modern American family often thinks of activities as the priority and plans mealtime accordingly. If your family is like mine, kids are often practicing sports or involved in other activities until the evening. This is simply our reality as a modern, busy household. The challenge is to not lose sight of the family meal as a priority most nights of the week. It may have to happen later than desired in the evening, or it may require cutting back on certain activities. I remember my mom feeding us a very large snack so that we could wait to have dinner when my dad got home at 7 p.m. This year I implemented "family dessert" when we were not able to have dinner together. At 8 p.m., I'd break out the ice cream sundaes and we'd talk and share. If a parent works swing shift, why not make breakfast the family meal? Whatever the cost, it's worth it! The family table matters and is worth guarding.

Meals are not simply for eating, but provide an opportunity to instill a sense of morality and family values. Our biggest influence is often time around the table. It offers the chance to develop minds, character, and emotional intelligence. When we establish rituals and traditions around the table, it becomes the heart of family life in the home. While you may get absorbed in the logistics of getting a meal on the table most evenings, keep the big picture in mind. We pause, gather, and grow at the table. Whether the meal is a fabulous homemade delicacy or cheese quesadillas with apple slices and carrot sticks, your family is sitting together, giving attention to each other, and saying that *family matters*.

While time at the table is important for reclaiming your family, remember that children will very seldom seem to appreciate or acknowledge your efforts. Though I'd like to pretend that everyone comes to my table gushing over the meal, more often than that not, they are more concerned about who is going to have to do dishes that night. Think back when you were a child. Most likely you were oblivious to the time and energy that went into putting together a meal. You just ate—probably complaining about the cooked vegetable on the plate in between bites. There is no cheering section as we deliver lasagna to the table. Our why is much deeper than the praise—it's the long-term hope that our faithfulness to this daily act will grow deep roots that support those gathered for years to come. Time at the table can be an integral part of reclaiming home, as it provides a venue for the foundational principles of love, acceptance, communication, play, and presence.

While most of us understand the importance, even demonstrated by research, of the family meal, it is still a struggle to make it happen every blessed night. We know what we *should* do, but it's just plain hard to be the one responsible to put it on the table 365 days a year, to make the grocery bill stretch, and to create a happy-family ambiance at the same time. The burden of the responsibility steals the joy out of the experience, and we frantically race off to the store or the drive-through window at 5 p.m. to put something … anything … on the table. I will not make any false promises that this struggle is going away—I've ended up in tears on family nights because it has all turned so, so wrong. But as we decide to reclaim the table some planning can help make dinnertime more manageable and less hectic, so that we can fully enjoy this nightly ritual. If we can solve the problem of *how*, then we are on our way to the more meaningful moments we desire.

Let's move from stressful to successful with ideas for mealtime solutions. Don't be overwhelmed by the number of ideas, just pick one or two that work for you and implement them. Also check online for more meal topics like budgets, recipes, and plans. There are entire websites that are devoted to helping you in this area. The following ideas might not solve all your mealtime issues, but if you can plan for your hardest days of the week, that is a great start.

MEAL PLANNING IDEAS:

Have a Dinner Plan by 10 a.m.

When you take the "think-work" out of the dinner quandary, it becomes a much easier process. When I wake up in the morning, I look at the whiteboard to see what I slated for dinner, and start preparing. If we are grilling, I set out the meat from the freezer to make sure it is thawed. If it's lasagna, I get it in the oven early so that it is fully cooked by the time my family gets home (no more waiting on the frozen lasagna). The crockpot is a favorite—I just put the ingredients in and let it do its thing all day long. I also set out the side dish and prepare the salad. If it's rice, I measure and have it sitting by the rice cooker. If it's pasta, I lay it next to the water in the pan on the cooktop. For salad, I prepare the greens at the beginning of the week and keep them rolled in towels in a plastic bag to save prep time.

Whatever your method, have it done before you leave for work, or before 10:00 a.m. Here's why: Dinnertime is usually go-time for parents. If you have young kids, they are usually needy late in the day just when you need to be preparing the meal. If the kids are older, you most likely are running carpool around this time, so there isn't time to prepare for dinner during the 4 p.m. to 7 p.m. block. When we are prepared, we save ourselves from the last minute scramble, save money, and have the satisfaction of providing a healthy meal for our family.

Cook and Freeze Meat

One very simple idea to get dinner on the table is to cook and freeze chicken, ground beef, or fish in bulk. Separate into small bags. When you need a quick meal, pull out the meat of choice, then add it to vegetables, pasta, a taco bar, or rice.

Double Meals

When cooking a meal, double or triple the recipe. Eat one meal for dinner, and then freeze the other meals for a later date. This can be done with breakfast dishes, cookies, cinnamon rolls, and desserts also.

Keep Ingredients for a "Go To" Recipe on Hand

There are certain meals that become family favorites, or simply reappear week after week because they are easy to make. Keep the ingredients for these meals on hand. When in a pinch, you have the peace of knowing there is an option that doesn't require forethought. For me, this meal is homemade pizza. I make the dough in the bread maker and put out marinara sauce, cheese, and pepperonis. Done!

Make Freezer Meals with a Cooking Group

This has been the most helpful tool I have found for the dinner dilemma. First, the extra hands are essential when assembling meals, which is why I recommend working with a group over preparing freezer meals individually. You can make more meals in a shorter amount of time. Second, it puts it on the calendar and gets done. We all have great intentions, but actually doing it is quite another matter. This ensures that we make time for bulk cooking. Third, it's economical. Last minute meals or going out to dinner are not cheap. We consume healthier food for a fraction of the cost when we eat at home.

Beyond that, there is not a price tag for the feeling of having a meal ready to pull out for dinner that is *already prepared*. I can't even express to you the stress it removes from my life, especially in this stage where I am carpooling kids to activities most afternoons or evenings. It's amazing! In many areas, there are businesses designed to help people make freezer meals, and several websites offer full menus, grocery lists, and meal plans. This method of cooking is also fun. Since we all have to feed our families, why not cook together?

If a cooking group does not appeal to you, there are other shared-meal options.

Organize a Meal Swap

This method involves inviting three other people to meal swap once a month. It differs from cooking group because you make the meals alone and then bring them to the designated place to trade dinners. This involves cooking two dishes multiplied by four. For example, if a person is making chicken and flank steak, she would make four chicken meals, and four flank steak meals, one for each family. You ultimately make eight meals total, and you go home with eight different meals (two from each person). You may specify that each person has to make one meat-based meal, and one pasta-based, or whatever special rules the group decides.

Start a Neighborhood Cooking Rotation

This method takes the neighborly concept to a whole new level. You pick one to three neighbors and designate a cooking night for each person. If I have Mondays, for example, I would cook dinner for my family, plus the other families in the group on that night. I would also deliver the meal to them on this night. On the other nights that I am not cooking, I get a meal delivered to me. This system works well for moms with young kids who aren't driving carpool during the late afternoon. It works best if everyone is in the same neighborhood, otherwise the driving and delivering is too much of a time drain.

Involve Kids in Cooking

This idea is not a time-saver, but it a great way to get a meal on the table and to spend quality time with kids. It will be messier, and more hassle, but it will also be instilling lifelong skills that they will carry into adulthood. A child is also more likely to eat what he has made himself … a bonus! Some fun ideas with kids include theme dinners, international cuisine, and, of course, basic kid favorites.

Ideas for Creating Meaningful Mealtimes

Now that we've looked at how we get a meal on the evening table, let's think through how to make dinnertime more meaningful.

- *Make electronics off-limits.*
  Have a device-free zone around the table—this includes all phones, computers, televisions, or any other device.
- *Agree on table protocol.*
  Establish in advance what the expectations are at the table. For example, you may want to practice having one person speak at a time. When our kids were little, we would pass a wooden frog around. Whoever had the frog was the only one who had permission to speak. If you didn't have the frog, it wasn't your turn to share. Though our kids are older, we still break out that frog when people are not listening well. Make sure everyone knows what is allowed, and what is not.
- *Refrain from discipline in the dining space.*
  The table is a place we want to be filled with warm, cozy memories. If you do have to address a disciplinary issue, take the child away from the meal, then return afterwards. Protect the table as a sanctuary. During one period when our kids were struggling with respect for one another during mealtime, we gave each child three tokens. Each time they did something to interrupt the peace of mealtime, we took one of their tokens. If they lost all three, they were stuck with dinner dishes. If they didn't, they got dessert. The extra motivation was very helpful.

- *Begin each meal with gratitude.*
  We often do not stop throughout a day and reflect on the gifts in our lives. Mealtime is a natural place to practice thankfulness. Pause, take a deep breath, clasp hands and offer thanks to God. Vary the prayers. Sometimes sing, other times read a verse, challenge everyone to sit in silence for one minute with a bowed head. If you are not coming from a place of faith, offer a toast instead of a prayer. Let's teach our kids that having warm food and shelter is a gift, a privilege that many people in the world do not enjoy. Another idea is to have each person around the table say something for which they are grateful.

- *Talk about a high, a low, and a betcha didn't know.*
  Each person shares something from the day that was a highlight, a "high." Then he/she shares something that was not so great, a "low." The "betcha didn't know" is something that was interesting or unusual. With younger children, it is sometimes helpful to begin with a personal story about a challenge you faced during your day, then ask them what was hard for them. The context allows them to understand the question better.

- *Talk about a current event and have everyone share his or her thoughts about it.*
  These can be tailored to the ages of your kids. Young kids can discuss lighter topics about your town, what is happening in the world, and funny animal stories. Older kids are ready to tackle more involved situations and issues. This kind of dinner table discussion develops their critical thinking skills and helps children form opinions.

- *Read a short story.*
  Take advantage of the captive audience at the table and read a story. Everyone can quietly eat while they listen. When my kids were young and at home, I would read chapters of classic books

out loud over lunch. For breakfast, we read a story that teaches a spiritual lesson. Over dinner, I often break out *Chicken Soup for the Soul* stories. Sharing a well-written tale together is a connector, and it spurs great discussion.

- *Draw conversation starters from a question jar.*
Keep a jar full of interesting, thought provoking questions by the table, and have someone draw one at dinner. Everyone shares his or her answer. You can create your own, or buy one online.

- *Teach manners.*
Mealtime is a natural place to teach the manners our kids need to know to be respectful dinner guests. Make it fun by giving surprise rewards to those who are polite. We teach kids how to value others when we instruct them on manners. My kids are often short on manners, but I still make the effort with the hope that one day they will be considerate dinner guests.

- *Learn about other cultures.*
The table can be used as a place to learn about the traditions of other places in the world. For example, while you share Japanese noodles, you can discuss the trade, history, and landscape of Japan.

- *Keep preschool dinners short.*
Young children often don't have the attention span to enjoy long meals. Do your best to keep them brief. Talking and sharing while they eat is the best way to keep their focus on the family discussion.

HOSPITALITY

One of the other great benefits of being meal-ready is that you are able to open up your heart and home to others on a more regular basis. I've always defined entertaining as the more formal, dressed-up sister to hospitality. Entertaining means the house should be clean, the meal at least somewhat fancy, and the guests impressed. Hospitality, rather, is a warm feeling that one experiences because she is *at home in another's presence*. Hospitality beckons guests because it is arms open, smiles wide, and generosity abundant. The greatest compliment anyone could give me is to say that they feel at home in our space. That is the goal. Maya Angelou said, "People won't remember what you did. People won't remember what you said. But people will always remember the way you made them feel."

Hospitality nourishes relationships, and it also sets an example of generosity to our children. When we have meals readily available, it frees us up to be hospitable and to enlarge our world. One of my friends doesn't travel much with her family, but she brings all kinds of cultures to her table by inviting missionaries and international students to dinner. She builds an international community right in her own home! Another friend of mine makes it a point to have her daughter's volleyball team over to their house for dinner every season. She cooks, shares, and organizes—all in order to build the team's sense of community. Her daughter is learning about hospitality by example, and is growing in how to welcome people to her table.

So many families do not have meals around the table. When you offer your home as a refuge and place of safety it makes a difference in a person's life. Are there people in your life, or your kids' lives, who could benefit from your hospitality? If you have older kids, is your house a place where friends can come and feel at home? Have you created that "come on in—we want you here" atmosphere?

Every spring break growing up I would join the Rein family on their spring break excursions. Each child got to bring someone, and Katie, the special friend from my childhood that I mentioned before, always chose me. There were seven children, so that was no small thing to let their kids invite someone along. Geri, the mom, was an amazing cook and put out feasts each night for fourteen kids, plus adults. But she didn't just put a meal on the table; she served it with an overjoyed smile and attitude, so happy to have all of us there. Looking back, I can't believe how much work that was for her... *on her vacation*! Geri modeled hospitality in the most compelling way. She is one of the reasons I grew to love the table.

Geri took hospitality on the road, and we can do that in many ways. When a meal is available in the freezer, we can deliver one when a need suddenly arises. Hospitality doesn't always have to be accompanied by food, but there is a reason it often goes hand in hand. Eating it is a basic need. When we are experiencing something difficult, this simple necessity becomes a giant burden. It is enough of a strain to sort through heavy emotions. Decisions like what to put on the table for the family become overwhelming. For this reason, offering food as a show of love and care is one of the most practical ways we can help each other in times of crisis. In doing so, you are also helping that family gather together during a time where keeping this ritual is vital for stability and comfort.

There is something sacred about coming together—even when we are frazzled, even when we are flipping simple grilled cheese sandwiches, even when we don't feel like it. Whether you are a kitchen gourmet straight off the pages of Pinterest, or the kind who cooks Hamburger Helper out of a box, you too can offer a family table that is a refuge of love and safety for all who sit and gather.

That is exactly what my Costa Rican host family did on that day long ago when I looked the pig in the eye. I pushed back from that Central American meal and sighed contentedly as the rain pounded the tin roof. A single candle flickered and danced, warding the mosquitoes away. The voices around me spoke in a language I did not fully comprehend, but their hearts wrapped me in a blanket of comfort, sharing with me the one thing they could offer: their table.

RECLAIMING THE TABLE
dares

• Write out what you will have for dinner for the next 3 days. Commit to prepping or organizing before you leave the house in the morning.

• Sit down and consider how to make meal planning easier for you.

• Read about a current event and discuss opinions at the dinner table. If you have young kids, read a short children's book and talk about the characters.

• Have a family discussion about table expectations.

• Find a new prayer or practice a fresh way to express gratitude at the table.

Chapter 9

RECLAIMING
TRADITIONS

*Enjoy the little things in life, for one day you may
look back and realize they were the big things.*
–Robert Breault

*The purpose of life, after all, is to live it, to taste experience to the utmost,
to reach out eagerly and without fear for newer and richer experience.*
–Eleanor Roosevelt

I f you dropped by my house sometime at the end of September, when the leaves have turned to a golden yellow and the air has grown crisp, you may find a couple hundred people in my yard. Every fall my sister's family joins mine in hosting a *Hootenanny*. Crockpots brimming with soup and chili sit on tables decorating our yard. Autumn-inspired desserts perch in another area, while treats made by kids sit in yet another section. Adult and kid judges carefully scrutinize the tasty fare, and record the cook-off results on scoring sheets neatly positioned on clipboards while bluegrass music plays happily in the background.

Kids bob for apples in an old galvanized laundry wash bin, and others jump in potato sack races. Because my sister's friends live in Washington, just west of where we live in Idaho, we do a Washington versus Idaho tug of war that is hands down the biggest competition of the day. Moms, dads, and kids all join in to pull down the rival. After the games, everyone eats, sips hot cider, and decorates pumpkins with pinecones, leaves, berries, and other woodland objects.

My sister and I run amok, tagging food for judging, refilling lemonade containers, snapping pictures, and doling out prizes. We love the crazy. It is one day of the year where communities gather together for old-fashioned fun. The party offers whispers of both days gone by, and the best is yet to come. Moms tell me that this annual harvest celebration has become as important to their kids as Christmas. They plan their entire month around it to make sure they are able to attend. There is no one more tied to this party than our own kids. It's become both a community and family tradition. While this might sound like magazine-article perfection, it isn't. There are spilled plates, hurt feelings about not winning the cook-off, bumps, accidental missed invitations, and tears when the rabbits at the petting zoo scratch. It isn't a perfect day, but it is our day, a celebration unique to our family and our community.

Traditions like the Hootenanny anchor us. They offer something that money can never buy—security, roots, and a sense of belonging in the world. Spinning a web of inter-connectedness in families and communities, they offer a valuable sense of identity. As we look at how to reclaim our homes, traditions may not seem at first glance to be a significant solution, but look again. These rituals communicate a value placed on our people—the ones we've been given in this life. They create memories, and become a part of the grand family story being written. When everyone feels a part of that story, unity grows. This births family identity, which is critical in crafting a sense of home and belonging. Family traditions are a tangible way to express the principles of reclaiming home. Traditions model the love, acceptance, communication, play, and presence that are embodied in each family and home.

CREATING MINI-TRADITIONS

We often think traditions need to be big, organized occasions. Those have a place and I am often willing to volunteer to host a grand soiree, but most of the time it is the small traditions that we adhere to consistently that mean the most. And because they are smaller and more doable, we often are more likely to stick to them. Mini-traditions are simply actions we do consistently with our families. The repetition over time and the unique nature of our family is what makes them a tradition. Nothing fancy or elaborate—just a little bit of fun and zest in the daily rhythm of life.

Children often lead in creating mini-traditions. For example, we aren't big on allowing our kids to drink soda, but I decided one day a couple of years ago that they could enjoy one with the pizza we traditionally have on Friday nights. The next Friday they asked for soda again. After two times, they coined Fridays pizza and pop night. To this day, it continues to be one of their favorites. Traditions don't have to be fancy or complicated——pizza and pop is nothing special and doesn't require any work on my part. Yet, it sets an anchor for my kids each week. If your family really likes something, they will want to repeat it. Allow your children to create some of the traditions that become a part of your family's story.

Another one of our weekly traditions is family night. This is simply one evening a week that is set-aside for a nice family dinner and activity. Sometimes it is a memorable night full of learning, conversation, fun games, and rich food. Other times simple soup fills the bowls and it totally flops. Either way, it is a tradition we practice week after week. My kids will probably not remember the family night lessons as much as the fact that it is a part of being a Gilbert. While it isn't easy to build this ritual into our week, we find a slot and put it on the calendar, even if that means other commitments need to be shuffled or deleted all together. It's what we do, and it communicates what we value.

CREATING UNIQUE TRADITIONS

Each New Year's Eve, my family loads the last chair up to the midway point of the mountain at a ski resort. As we click off our bindings to climb the rest of the way up the ridge in our ski boots, the ski patrol makes their yearly speech disclaiming any responsibility for us. Cousins, sons, daughters, aunts, uncles, moms, dads, and friends kick step up the steep slope, encouraging each other when it gets tough. Waiting at the top are thermoses of hot chocolate and friendly smiles from the fittest and fastest among us. We prop up our skis and rest, leaning against them, sipping the warmth.

After a while, my cousin, Ian, sets off Roman candles when the night skiing lights go out. That signifies it is almost time to light the flares. Each person gets two flares and we light them one by one, careful to hold them away from each other. One person takes the lead and we ski down in a snakelike fashion, follow the leader style, creating a ski torchlight parade. "Happy New Year!" rings through the air as we usher in January with the warmth of community and the rejuvenation of being on a mountaintop.

We are proud of this tradition. It sets us apart as a family. Anyone is welcome to come, but most of the time it is just us with a few good family friends thrown in and, every once in a while, a stranger or two. This is how we mark New Year's Eve as a family. It's different. Our kids will grow up reminiscing about the hike and knowing it is a part of their

Ideas for mini Traditions:

SUNDAY SUNDAES

HOUR OF POWER
(Saturday morning clean up after cartoons)

SUNDAY MORNING HOG & JOG
(a morning run followed by breakfast out)

FULL MOON MADNESS
(stay up late and have special drinks, or take a hike,
on a full moon)

TALENT SHOW TUESDAY
(kids perform skits, talents, show -n- tells, etc.)

FIRESIDE CHAT
(read a classic novel to the family by the fire, or pick a
topic of conversation or current event and discuss)

WING-STOP WEDNESDAY OR TUESDAY TACOS:
One-on-one dates bi-weekly or weekly

continued . . .

Ideas for mini Traditions:

FUN FRIDAY AFTER SCHOOL ACTIVITY

MONDAY MUFFINS

HIKE & HAMBURGERS
(after exploring, go eat at a local hamburger favorite)

FRIDAY NIGHT LIGHTS
(ultimate frisbee, football, soccer, golf,
capture the flag, or baseball games)

POP & POKER NIGHT

FLIP FLOP LEMON DROP PICNICS
(homemade lemonade, blankets on the
front lawn, flip flops, lemon drop candy)

THE BIRTHDAY HAT
(Pick a sombrero or another large hat for the
birthday person to wear on the special day.)

unique story. In thinking through family celebrations, consider adding a unique tradition to your year.

These four elements will help you create a unique family tradition:

1. *The element of challenge*—overcome something.
2. *The element of connection*—embark on an experience that will draw you closer to one another.
3. *The element of fun*—enjoy the activity. Try to make the fun element stronger than the challenge element. Sometimes this means there is a big reward at the end.
4. *The element of originality*—choose something unique that not every family does.

Some Ideas:
- Turning thirteen adventure
- Summer backpacking trip
- Canoe or kayak day trip on Labor Day
- Pie baking extravaganza in October for neighbors
- Family Olympics on the first day of summer break
- Family snowshoe on January 1
- Smokestack party (pick another family, stack each other's wood before winter, then have a party)! Other variations include pulling up the garden, raking the yard, or trimming trees.

HOLIDAY TRADITIONS

Holidays provide built-in places to include tradition in our year. The quirky little actions we do over and over during these seasons create ritual and wonder. Sitting in a prominent place in our kitchen at Christmastime, our advent calendar holds a box for each day of December. The kids take turns opening the container and pulling out the slip of paper designated for that date. Written on the note is the activity for the day. Sometimes it says we're going to leave treats at a neighbor's door then run away. Other times it reads, "Watch a Christmas special with European hot chocolate." The anticipation of each slip of paper promising a break from the normal routine of life makes this tradition special.

This year I used the season of Lent, the days leading up to Easter, to establish a new tradition. Wanting to offer opportunities for my kids to grow more in faith, I set up a prayer station at a small table in our living room. At the station was a Bible, a candle, a verse of the day, and a prayer journal. Each morning, sometime before leaving the house, each child was to visit the center. He'd light the candle, read the verse, and pray. Did it happen everyday? No. But it did sometimes, and it did make the season leading up to Easter more meaningful.

Rather than seeing holidays as a time of stress and financial drain, harness them for creating family identity and for passing down values. If certain holidays are overwhelming, simply pick one simple tradition and follow through with it. Every little step is a move that deepens family roots.

While tradition implies that the activity is repeated every year, sometimes flexibility is in order. I have vivid memories of my kids groaning through the mall as I dragged them onto Santa's lap. Growing up, my family had a Santa picture taken every year. My mom proudly displayed them at Christmas and we loved seeing the changing styles and faces through the festive collection. For some reason, my brother, sister, and I embraced the ritual. My kids did not. Every minute they had to wear nice clothes and sit on the jolly man's lap was torture.

One December, as I was preparing for yet another trudge to the local North Pole, I began to laugh uncontrollably. My boys stood in their itchy sweaters and looked at me miserably. My daughter pulled at her sparkly dress and frowned. Why was I forcing them to do a tradition they couldn't stand just because that is what I had done growing up? I liked the photos, but it was not a huge priority to me. There were other traditions I cared much more about doing that we all enjoyed. I waved the white flag and gave up that particular family tradition.

Admittedly, there are (many) times when kids are going to have to do something just because that is what we want them to do, whether they like it or not. But let's remain flexible and ask ourselves and other family members, "Is this a tradition that we all enjoy? Is this still important to me? Is it still important to anyone else in the family?" Families with young children may find that certain traditions are magical, and create a sense of wonder and joy. The kids may outgrow some of these traditions eventually, and new ones will replace those once so important.

HOLIDAY FAMILY FIGHTS

While holidays are often a time of joy, they can also be painful and full of dread. Whether you are mourning the loss of someone important, or navigating very complex family dynamics, the holidays are a time when emotions and expectations skyrocket.

All of us carry a suitcase full of ideas containing unspoken rules about how celebrations and traditions ought to be lived out and with whom. The conflicts range from when to open Christmas presents to whether or not to invite certain family members to the holiday table. There is potential for blazing fireworks of conflict, strife, and hurt feelings.

While some of this is inevitable, we can set up the holidays for success as best as possible:

Plan Well—Hold a family meeting in the early fall to thoroughly discuss the holiday schedule. Review where you will spend your time and who will be with you. It is important to *identify potential problems and then find a coping strategy.*

One of my friends knows that she can't spend more than three days with her in-laws or relationships start to suffer. With that knowledge, she plans accordingly during the holidays. Another friend has a very difficult mother who asks to spend Christmas with her. While bringing her into their home on Christmas Day would be potentially disastrous, my friend does want to honor her mother. The compromise is she celebrates their "Christmas" together a few days before the actual day. The key to planning well is to realistically assess the dynamics of relationships, and then make decisions based on that assessment.

Planning ahead of time also gives families an opportunity to hash out differences before the emotion of the moment. It is often difficult to blend traditions between people who may have grown up very differently. For example, one of my friends likes a quiet, simple, small Christmas day with just her family. Her husband wants a room bursting with extended family and a festive feast. Each year they have to come to an agreement and compromise on how to spend that day.

A woman in my community recently went through a painful divorce. She will plan new experiences and travels this Christmas to distract her kids from the pain of their family situation. Planning ahead of time allows us to anticipate well and set our holidays up for success.

Communicate—While not everyone will agree with the arrangements you have made, tell others what you have decided and stick to the plan. This honors others by keeping them informed, which is respectful. Initiating also benefits you because the proposed plan has been carefully weighed and considered.

Keep Cool—No matter how much you have planned for success, there may be a difficult situation or moment that arises due to strong personalities. While you can't control them, you can control yourself. If needed, excuse yourself from the area. Take a walk, go to the bathroom, drive to the store, or sit in the backyard. Most likely old conflicts will not have new endings. Often there is no win in fighting back in this setting. You may need to address your differences another time, sometimes with help, but the holiday table is probably not the place for resolving conflict.

Holiday Tradition Ideas

Thanksgiving Traditions

Put each name on a piece of cardstock and set them at a place setting around the table with a pen. Have each person write why they are grateful for that person on their paper. When each goes to sit down, they have a whole paper filled up with loving words and thoughts. This can also be done with a marker on small pumpkins set at each place.

Create a "Grateful Tree." Put some branches in a large vase. Cut up squares of paper and hole punch the ends. Have each person write 3 things for which they are thankful and hang them on the tree.

During the meal prayer, have each person give thanks to God for something in his or her life.

Participate in a Turkey Trot fun run or host a Turkey Bowl football game at a park.

Deliver a Thanksgiving meal to someone in need.

Show up on someone's doorstep to simply tell them how thankful you are for him/her in your life. Add cookies or pumpkin pie if you want!

Christmas Traditions

Decorate human Christmas trees using green crepe paper, ornament hooks, balls, tinsel, and garland (the person is the tree).

Read a new Christmas book each day, either from your own collection or from the library. Turn off all of the lights except the Christmas tree and settle in for the tale.

Learn the words to a Christmas carol each week.
When the 25th nears, go caroling at a retirement center.

Host a holiday party in your yard with
sleds, lanterns, and a cocoa bar.

Visit a live nativity and talk about it afterwards with your kids.

Give a gift from Jesus on Christmas Eve.
Make it a present that is faith-related.

Ding, dong, Christmas ditch your neighbors,
leaving a plate full of goodies on their doorstep.

Collect change in a jar all year long. At Christmastime,
leave it on someone's porch. *The Christmas Jar* is
a book that goes along with this tradition .

Valentine's Traditions

Put small mailboxes for each family member on the kitchen counter for the month of February. Encourage the family to write each other notes and to put little surprises inside.

Have a special Valentine's dinner with candlelight, and at each place leave a note that says, "5 Reasons Why I Love You."

Have a candy-heart stacking contest. See who can pile the most candy hearts on top on each other, creating towers. Another variation is to create candy heart "forts."

Dine on chocolate fondue fireside.

Make heart shaped cookies and decorate them with icing, sprinkles, and candy hearts. Enjoy as a family or give as gifts.

Easter Traditions

Send the kids on an Easter basket scavenger hunt. Hide notes that lead them to their baskets . Add books to the basket in addition to candy.

Watch "The Passion of the Christ" movie together and discuss.

Deliver Easter lilies to people in the hospital or senior living center.

Go around the table and have each person read a part of the resurrection story from the Bible, or listen to it on a children's audio program if you have younger children.

Have an adult Easter egg hunt. Hide money in the eggs. Make a couple of the eggs big hitters, and put small change in the others.

Hide 12 eggs in someone's yard.
Leave a note sending them on the hunt.

Invite someone to go to church with you,
and surprise him/her with a bouquet of daffodils.

Make a birdfeeder using pinecones, peanut butter, and seeds.
Talk about spring and new beginnings.

Fourth of July Traditions

Attend a small town parade and dress up in
red, white, and blue.

Have a picnic in the park and play Frisbee or bocce ball
until the firework show.

Go to a lake in your area and boat or canoe out to the
middle of the lake to watch fireworks.

Thank a veteran in some way and talk about
the freedoms you enjoy with your family.

Invite friends or family over for
Bingo, BBQ, & banana splits.

Read the Declaration of Independence out loud as a family

Watch an online video about the history of the fourth of July.

Line your driveway with miniature flags.

See who can write down the original
13 colonies first. Give a prize to the winner.

BIRTHDAYS

A few years ago, my sister and I brainstormed a meaningful way to usher in my nephew, Caleb's, thirteenth birthday. It is a milestone age for everyone. Both children and parents come face-to-face with new realities. The climb up the mountain of the teen years requires new equipment, endurance, a route map, and a team. There are obstacles ahead, but also breathtaking vistas along the way.

The thirteenth birthday marks the beginning of this expedition. It's base camp. Base camp is where climbers prepare for their journey. Here supplies are stocked, packs are prepared, and the warm security of safety is found. As Kendra and I talked about what to do, we wanted to create something memorable; something to fill his pack, to offer him an experience he could look back on when the climb gets tough, or when he just needs to know that the safety of base camp remains.

We decided to have him walk a path to a favorite creek down a dirt road by the family lake cabin. Along the way he would encounter family members who would tell him something that sets him apart as unique and special, and offer him a gift. It would also be an opportunity for the adults in his life to share some of their wisdom.

On his birthday, my sister revealed the plan. He was told that people would meet him, and that each would walk him to the next person. After everyone was in place, his dad gave him a bag to hold each symbolic gift he would receive, and sent him on his walk. What he found was his grandpa giving him advice and wisdom about how to handle money, his uncle telling him why he is five-star, his cousin explaining why he is a role model in his life, his grandma discussing the importance of legacy, and his aunt reminding him to stand on a firm foundation. As he wound through the tall grass down the final path to the creek, the extended family greeted him on the bridge with cheers and shouts. With the smell of summer washing over us, and with praise on our lips, we laid hands on Caleb's shoulders and opened our hearts in earnest prayer.

We petitioned God to walk with him, to shape him into a young man of integrity, and to protect his heart. A younger cousin, in total adoration, jumped in his arms at the final "amen." It was a great birthday—one that provided strong roots for his life.

In a couple of short weeks, my almost thirteen year old, Dawson, will walk that same road. He is an aspiring writer, so instead of objects, we are going to give him books that hold wisdom, faith, and significance. Each person will inscribe their message to him on the inside of a book, as well as speak it to him on the path. As with Caleb, no doubt it will be a beautiful example of mentoring, celebration, family, and legacy.

Every human heart wants to be known and deeply loved. Birthdays provide an opportunity for us to practically demonstrate that kind of care. We get to single someone out, and shower them with a kindness that makes an impact. Not every birthday will be an extravagant occasion like the one mentioned above, but birthdays provide an opportunity to love well and to water the soul planted in the garden of family. Let's not miss that chance.

Birthday Ideas:

- Sixteen surprises for a sweet sixteen: Throughout the day, flood your sixteen year old with little (or big) surprises. If it is a school day, arrange pizza delivery at lunch for her and all of her friends.
- The Bistro: Make a special dinner and dessert every year for the birthday child (their favorite).
- The Birthday Hot Seat: Create a "hot seat" in the middle of the room. The birthday boy wears a crazy hat that is for birthdays only, and everyone tells him what they love about him.
- The Kidnap: Kidnap the birthday kid from school and go out to lunch.
- The Cake Smash: When the birthday boy blows out the candles, smash his head into the cake. Afterwards you can tell him why

he is so smashing! This happened to my son when he celebrated his birthday in Costa Rica one year. It is a tradition there. He loved it!

- Balloon Bomb: Fill a box, a car, or a room with balloons filled with special notes and money.
- The Auntie Date: Take your nieces or nephews on a special one-on-one date for their birthday. It's rare that an aunt or uncle gets that kind of quality time. When possible, I do this with my nieces (I have eight of them), and I treasure that time.
- Talent Tip: Take your child to a class, or to a place that will encourage a special interest on their birthday. Spend the whole day doing what they love with them.
- The Hidden Cupcake: Fill a ceramic cupcake, or other container, with a surprise. Hide it somewhere in the house. Have the birthday girl or boy go hunting for it.

SUMMER

There is one summer tradition that serves as therapy for my entire year: huckleberry picking. We hunt through the forest with galvanized pails swinging from eager hands, searching for bushes that droop heavy laden from the weight of plump, succulent berries. When we find a bountiful area, our lips are sealed, keeping the location secret. Good huckleberry pickers have several spots that belong to them alone. Our kids puff out their chests, as if standing on a podium, as they reveal the amount picked that day. We gather our yield together and measure out bags for the freezer, careful not to miss one single berry. Throughout the year, on only the most special occasions, we mix them into crisps, parfaits, and pies. We hear echoes of those sun-soaked treks through the woods as we savor the sweet and sour flavor throughout the year.

Summertime beckons all of us to pause and take in the wonder of life all around. Whether it is turning berries into jam, camping along the creek, or gathering family and friends for a backyard barbeque, this season invites connection and tradition. The challenge is making sure these are not pushed aside by other commitments. At the beginning of each summer, Erik and I sit down and block out space on the calendar for our most important traditions. The summer weeks go by too quickly. Learning how to schedule wisely is one of the best ways to ensure that we make the most of this treasured season.

Planning the Best Summer Yet

- *List all of the required activities and events and put them on the calendar.* These are non-negotiable items (weddings, family reunions, sports tryouts, etc.). Ours this year are my husband's work commitments, a family gathering at the lake, high school soccer tryouts, football tryouts.

- *Brainstorm and make a list of those activities you want to take priority on the summer schedule.* These are the fun items, the "memory makers." For example, we are prioritizing a backpacking trip, a father/daughter adventure week, camping with cousins from Oregon, family camp, and a visit from close friends.

- *Put the priorities on the calendar.* And ... are you ready for this? DON'T MOVE THEM. If you've blocked out a week to be at home with the family for a staycation, then when your college roommate asks if she can come for a visit during those dates, you say "No, we are on vacation." Make them a priority in your mind and don't let other engagements shove them off the calendar.

- *Ask the kids what is important to them and put some of those items on the schedule.* Notice, this comes after the family priorities. Not only ask your children what is important to them, but also enlist their help to make those activities happen.

- *List the "extras" you want to do that haven't been put on the calendar.* You may be someone who likes unscheduled free time in the summer. I know it sounds counter-intuitive, but block out some days that are "scheduled" unscheduled time. These are reserved for the lemonade stand, ice cream truck, capture the flag, outdoor movie kind of days. With this approach, though the end of August will still sneak up, we can rest in the satisfaction of having spent our time well.

Summer Ideas:

- *Live Music:* Look in the paper to see where live music is in your area. Pack a picnic and enjoy a free summer concert on the lawn.
- *The Seven Wonders of our Town:* Instead of visiting the Seven Wonders of the World, visit the seven wonders of your town or region. Put them on the calendar and celebrate the place you live.
- *Camping:* Whether it is in your backyard or in the woods, pitch a tent, gaze at the stars, cook over an open fire, and make memories.
- *Hit the Road:* Rent an RV, drive to a favorite destination, or take a family bike ride to the best local ice cream spot.
- *Cousin Camp:* Set aside a few days to have all of the cousins together. Plan local outings, crafts, obstacle courses, and sleeping in backyard tents.
- *Lake Life:* Most people can find a body of water within driving distance. The lazy days of lake life bring out the best of summer. Pack the float toys and plenty of drinks.
- *Scream for Ice Cream:* Make the real stuff. Turn it by hand in an old-fashioned ice cream maker, or use the modern appliance to whip up this delicious treat.

- *Date your Spouse:* Summer is the perfect time to carve out romantic moments. Take a moonlight hike, picnic in the park, sleep under the stars, or dine by candlelight on the patio of your favorite restaurant.

RECLAIMING TRADITIONS
dares

• Pick a mini-tradition you would like to start implementing on a weekly or monthly basis in your home.

• Leave a treat on each person's pillow that reflects the season.

• Consider the traditions you do around the upcoming holiday. What traditions are meaningful and/or enjoyable? Which ones need to go?

• What specific action can you implement that would make birthdays more meaningful in your family?

• How do you want to change how you spend your summer to create more family time?

Chapter 10

RECLAIMING
LEGACY

The greatest legacy one can pass on to one's children and
grandchildren is not money or other material things accumulated
in one's life, but rather a legacy of character and faith.
–Billy Graham

Your tomb will have a birth and death with a dash
in the middle. What will you do with your dash?
–Bill Hybels

Rays of sunlight reflected off vases filled with flowers surrounding the cemetery. My Grandma would have been so happy to have us all together in one place—uncles sitting next to nephews, cousins next to great aunts. If people are able to smile down on us from heaven, I am sure that was a moment she did. As my mom kneeled to put flowers on her mother's grave and say her final goodbyes, my son, Hudson, only ten years old, stepped out from the crowd, walked up behind her, and placed his hands gently on her back. *This is heritage.* It is an invisible family line of connection that says, "You are not alone. We journey together."

Having grown up in close proximity to grandparents on both sides of the family, I hold in my mind a swirl of memories. Crab cocktail, Grandpa's fedora, and the Sunday pot roast all join in the menagerie. Of all my recollections, perhaps none are more vivid than our simple summers by the lake. On one particular holiday, I remember the handmade round table creaking as Grandma folded the mayonnaise into the potato salad. It was her specialty and the Fourth of July would not happen without it. The smell of burnt sparklers drifted over the lake accompanied by delighted laughs. Mom and several others harmonized by the blazing fire, while Dad bellowed out of tune next to her. I sat with my toes dangling into the water while feet scampered up and down the dock behind me. The glow of the fireworks reflected off the water and shone light upon all of the faces of my family. Three generations weaved and intertwined as harmoniously as the colors of the sunset that set in the western sky.

These sweet family moments make us want to stop time and hold onto the feelings forever. We realize that we belong to something sacred. That belonging has a significance that outlives our human existence. In it, countless legacies are left to those present and to future generations. Roots push deeply under the ground and grow up into solid, healthy trees.

Over time, action upon action, and word upon word, we pass down a combination of skills, behaviors, thought-patterns, spiritual truths, and ethics that equip future generations. They will stand on the experience we have built, and respond accordingly. A life coach once encouraged me to write my own eulogy then read it often. This action helps in making choices daily that align with how we want to live, and one day, be remembered. In the same way, to ensure that we are leaving the legacy we want to pass on, it is wise to begin with the end in mind by thinking through various components of legacy.

HERITAGE

Great Aunt Martha was the gardener, Uncle Latin the engineer turned preacher, Aunt Emma the Rice-Krispie-Treat baker extraordinaire, and Crazy Aunt Joanne the world traveler and modern-day Lucille Ball. Each weaved a piece of their heart into the fabric of mine. Quirky, flawed, and even sometimes inappropriate, they were also fun, lively, fiercely loyal, and kind. These were and are our people, and together create this thing we call family. Heritage is all that we inherit from this circle, and what we decide to pass down.

Heritage happens as we sit around the campfire and hear stories of Grandpa Jones, who ran the Boy Scout camp on Diamond Lake and could make even the most serious laugh. It happens as ten cousins sit around a table dealing cards, all aimed at beating their grandpa in poker. And it trickles into our hearts as we replay cousin Adam carrying his 200+ pound uncle, like a sack of potatoes, down the middle of the dance aisle at a family party. Being connected to something larger than ourselves gives us a sense of belonging in the world, a rootedness that produces security and identity.

Some do not live near family and creating a sense of heritage from afar is challenging. Others do not have the kind of family where this is possible. I have several friends who want nothing to do with their family's legacy, as it is full of alcoholism, abuse, and divorce. Even if this is your reality, you can still create heritage. Church family, close friends, and loyal neighbors can fill in that gap. My dear friend explains that because her family is so broken, she adopts her close friends as family.

Raising kids, celebrating milestones, and ringing in holidays happen with those friends who have become so dear.

All of our families are made up of human beings, who are broken and in need of redemption, but no question there are some who are much more challenging, and sometimes even impossible. If your family is very damaged, do your best to unearth the good part of your heritage. Most can find redeeming elements sprinkled through generations. Speak of those people and of the positive legacy they pass to your children. In this situation, the heritage piece may happen more by oral tradition than actual relationships.

Talking about the damaging threads of families can also be a way to redeem a broken heritage. One friend of mine began communicating to her children about the alcoholism that has plagued their extended family once the kids were at an age to maturely process the information. She informed them that the genes they carry leave them vulnerable to addiction. Using the painful experience of family history to teach her kids about the pitfalls of alcohol abuse, my friend transformed a negative heritage into a powerful life lesson.

Bringing to light family secrets also decreases shame. It takes away the power of the secrets. Another friend has a distinctive family history of anxiety and depression. Suicide has not been uncommon in his family. Knowing this from an early age, he sought intervention early when he saw signs in himself and in one of his children.

While we do not get to choose the heritage into which we've been born, we do get to choose what we pass on and what we don't. Rather than fearing our genetic or emotional legacy, let's approach *our* immediate families with the empowered mindset of courage and choice. If your childhood memories are stormy thoughts that you'd rather block out, remember that you get to reclaim legacy in the way that you choose for your own family. While we can't control what is in the past, or what we experienced in our family of origin, we can choose the parts we want to bring forward and weave into our children's experience. Likewise, we also get to choose how we want to make changes to our story, determining what it means to reclaim our legacy *going forward*.

If you do not identify with the above, but rather have healthy, life-giving relationships with extended family, that is a precious gift that many do not get to experience in this life. Treat it as the treasure that it is, clearing time in your schedule and making it a central part of your family's culture.

Combining two sets of heritage can be difficult. My friend, Alexandra, explains that her girls want to claim their Dutch heritage because of their last name and fair coloring, but she wants them to know that there is another half to their heritage also—hers. How do you honor one heritage while not letting it dominate?

In reality it can be difficult to create a perfectly equal celebration of both sides of the family. However, we can honor both and work to incorporate the positive parts from each. Talk through those parts of your heritage that are important with your spouse and decided how you will incorporate those into your family's life. It may be only on holidays, or around certain birthdays, but discussing them ahead of time creates room for both of you to be a part of the tradition.

Respecting the other's roots demonstrates honor and love, both of which create rich heritage in your family's life.

One special note to parents of adopted children: I realize the heritage piece can be complicated. A simple school assignment asking an adopted child to outline their family history or ancestry can cause a major breakdown and crisis. Handling these matters with an attitude of sensitivity and care is always a good starting place.

My niece is adopted from Russia. Every year on the day she was officially adopted, we celebrate her Russian roots with a "Gotcha Day." My sister has been known to make Russian stew, fill piñatas with Russian candy, and teach everyone Russian phrases. We pray over Olivia, her birth parents, and fully celebrate her cultural roots. Olivia's birth in Russia is a part of her story, and so is her adoption into our family. Both are important and need to be celebrated, so we do. Russia has been integrated into our family's heritage, and we now have a special place in our hearts for a country that before was just a dot on a map.

For some children, having a different starting place than the rest of the family can be painful. The more we can celebrate their unique story and use their place of origin as a meaningful addition to our family's heritage, the more children will be able to embrace their roots.

Practical Ways to Celebrate Family Heritage:

- **Collect family recipes and put them together in a book.** If you can copy recipes written in personal handwriting, even better. If there is room, write a few sentences about the person next to the recipe.
- **Gather old and new family pictures and create an album.** Flip through the album to tell about the characters that make up your clan.
- **Visit the country of your ancestors.** If traveling is not possible, host an evening dinner that tells of the culture and the food of that region. Learn about their traditions and the people. This is also a way to include cultural heritage for adopted children, or for family members who are no longer alive.
- **Plan a family of origin (FOO) trip.** It sometimes is too difficult or expensive to get everyone together. Plan to spend a weekend somewhere with the family you grew up in, therefore continuing to build and care for those relationships.
- **Gather around a campfire.** Have the adults tell stories of their parents, aunts, uncles, and grandparents.

- **Plan a reunion.** Gather your people and make it a priority on the calendar. Make sure there is an opportunity for people to ask questions and share stories.
- **Use family heirlooms and talk about their significance.** For example, my grandma gave me my great-great grandmother's crystal bowl for our wedding gift. It is over 200 years old. I use it and we talk about the dinner tables that have enjoyed this bowl through the years.
- **Pass down family traditions.** Little or big, these are significant to a family.
- **Make a family heritage photo wall.** Place the wonderful old photos in prominent places on the wall where you will talk often about the people who adorn the frames.
- **Visit the towns and houses where you grew up.** Explore family history by finding out where various people in your family were raised.
- **Learn and sing music that is special to your family.** Where words fail, music communicates. Whether it is quirky ballads, traditional hymns, or cultural rhythms, music is a joyful way to honor family heritage.

A PLACE TO CALL HOME

My father-in-law grew up in the tiny town of Sweet Home, Oregon. Every Memorial Day, his extended family gathers at the graveside of all who have gone before them. Afterwards, they caravan to the local park. Using a vintage family heirloom ice cream maker, people take turns churning the cream and adding the rock salt and ice. Aunt Suzanne lays out the tablecloth that has the name of every person in the family she hand embroidered onto it. All enjoy a hearty picnic. Though they don't own this piece of land to which they return, this place offers roots to

Heritage Questions

1. Which family members create a positive heritage for my family?

2. How can I spend more time cultivating relationships with those people?

3. What can I do to teach my children more about their family history?

4. How can I encourage relationships between generations? Does a family member have a skill she/he can teach a younger generation?

5. On the next holiday, how can I encourage traditions that celebrate our family history?

those who share in its beauty. They are reminded of family, heritage, and the value of both.

When we repeatedly go back to one place, over and over throughout our lifetimes, building memory upon memory, there is a fusing that occurs between that place and our hearts. If it is a location of natural beauty, combining nature and place, that powerful combination has double the impact. We associate peace, connection, and a sense of belonging. For some, it may be a park where they always share a picnic, a family cabin on a lake, for others, a certain campground, and others, maybe a special outcropping next to a river.

My husband asked me to marry him on the ski hill where I grew up. We ended up having our ceremony on that same mountain. That place holds countless memories for me, from my dad racing me down a ski run, to my husband down on one knee. So much of my story has been written there. It is woven into the fabric of my life indelibly, offering roots and grounding.

As we seek to offer those same roots to our children, think through incorporating place. Is there a location that you can return to every year to build memories? Is there a place of natural beauty that your family can enjoy together on a regular basis? In the *Reclaiming Childhood* chapter we talked about safe places for kids. The places I am talking about regarding legacy are places that we can experience as a family, and that become a location where important family memories are made. Sometimes these places are one and the same, sometimes they are different. As we seek to help our children find their story on this earth, where they come from, and who they are, place can be a powerful and positive element that helps shape family identity.

CREATING CULTURE

Every group, big or small, has its culture. If you've visited another country, you've seen the way people act and how they feel about being a part of that nation. There are certain norms, behaviors, and rituals that shape the people in that environment. As I mentioned before, in college I studied abroad and visited several countries in Europe. Over spring break, my friend, Jill, and I moved in with a family on the Greek island of Crete. During their Easter celebration, we sat at a long farm table in a community center, soaking in the culture of the Greeks. The six-hour dinner included toasts, chants, long chats, and an abundance of food. They spoke passionately and patted each other on the back with vigor. The Greek culture bubbles with zest for life, and the people reflect that value. That example is on a grand scale, but even small groups have a culture. Spend a practice or two with a soccer team and you'll learn their culture. Peer into the inner workings of a classroom, and you can identify a culture.

The same is true in our families. We create a culture. If you immediately think condemning thoughts, realizing the one that currently exists is not the culture you desire, push the pause button. There have certainly been seasons where, in my family, I have been discouraged by our culture. There have been times when it seemed that my kids couldn't be in the same room together without someone getting angry, hurt, or needled. Thankfully, every day is a new beginning to create what did not exist before this moment. This is the hope that each morning delivers. If you have not been a person of encouragement, start building others up today. If you have not created a positive mood in your home, begin creating it this minute. If you've been angry, decide to take a breath and try to be more patient. We can't change what has been, but we are in full control of what is *to be*.

What kind of culture do you want in your home? Nordstrom wants to be known as the store where the customer is treated with respect and care. Nike wants the title of sports leader in innovative athletic wear. What about you? For what do you want your family to be known? What is your family brand? Decide what it is and then start leading your family in that direction. Every group needs a leader who will set the example and spur others on toward the goal. That's YOU!

This idea of culture has shaped how I see my role in the home. Like a captain, I steer our ship and set its course. The crew is looking to me for direction and it's important I lead with skill and care. A culture will be created by default, so we are wise to consider what culture we are creating.

Take some time right now to answer the questions on the next page about the culture in your home:

FAMILY MISSION STATEMENTS

One of the best ways to evaluate the family culture is through mission statements. Mission statements are commonly used in successful businesses and corporations. This short idea drives their culture. It narrows the company's focus and reminds them what they are about and who they are at the core. When they face decisions, they ask, "Does this fit with our mission statement?" For example, Starbucks, the coffee culture trailblazer, has a mission statement that reads, "To inspire and nurture the human spirit—one person, one cup, and one neighborhood at a time." When they create their products and expand their company, this short sentence serves as a guide and ruler. Their primary goal is to inspire and nurture the human spirit, so this becomes the measure for their expansion.

Like good businesses, families need a mission statement—a short, memorable statement about the family's core values and purpose. It does not mean that other things outside of that are not good, but what is inside the mission statement is what is BEST, and where we want to focus our attention.

One definition of legacy is *a thing handed down by a predecessor.* Our job is to decide what it is we want to hand down. We may not want to pass everything down, so we must choose those things we deem most valuable. The first step in creating a mission statement is

Home Culture

Take some time right now to answer these questions about the culture in your home:

1. Write 3 words that describe the current culture of your home:

2. When you walk in the door of your home, how do you want to feel (the general atmosphere)?

3. What 3 attitudes do you want to see among the people in your family?

4. What 3 behaviors do you want to witness in the home on a regular basis?

5. What 3 core values are most important as a family?

6. How can you be a better leader in creating a positive family culture?

brainstorming what is most important. Take a moment to look back at Chapter 2 and the values you listed as most important in evaluating time commitments. These values can feed into your thinking on legacy and your family mission statement.

Set aside time to answer the question:

What are the three most important legacies I can leave to my children and to their children?

Some ideas include:

- A spiritual heritage
- A strong work ethic
- How to treat others with dignity and respect
- Skills in the outdoors
- Spending time as a family
- Dreaming big
- Stepping out of one's comfort zone
- Developing confidence
- Business skills
- How to run a home
- How to cook
- How to celebrate well
- Creating traditions
- Serving the poor
- Developing a global perspective
- Music appreciation

Write down the top three legacies you want to pass on to your children:

1.

2.

3.

Take the three legacies you wrote down and see if you can put them together into a phrase. For example, for my family our top three values are:

A spiritual heritage
Family unity
Living with integrity

There are other traits we value, but these reign supreme. Our family mission statement reads: "Honor God. Love others. Live with integrity." Because of our faith, we also chose a scripture that we have claimed as our family verse, 1 Peter 4:8-11.

Andy Stanley, who has taught extensively on vision and leadership, says that the best statements are those that are "memorable, repeatable, and portable—those that roll off the tip of your tongue." Keep this in mind as you brainstorm. It is hard to remember anything longer than a sentence or two. We want our children to be able to call this statement to mind when they are in a situation that requires a decision. Likewise, parents find a simple sentence flows more naturally when in the middle of correcting, encouraging, or disciplining. Write out your family's mission statement.

My grandpa was a small business owner who made deals on a handshake. There was never a question that, as part of the family, we were to do the same in life. He didn't have to explain what it meant. We knew. Be honest, a person of your word, trustworthy, honoring of others, dependable, and hard working. When my kids eventually move into a life of their own, my hope is that our family mission statement will serve as a reminder of our family's core values, just like Grandpa's handshake.

Legacy embraces the aspects of your family history that you choose to keep and incorporate. It also blazes new heritage, forging

solid roots through family culture and mission statements that *you* create.

FAMILY INTERVIEWS

My parents sat next to each other on red Adirondack chairs at the family cabin, finishing each other's sentences. The familiar creak of the dock and the waves lapping onto the beach provided comforting background noise for my parent's narration.

I was conducting a family history interview to give to my siblings and their families for a homemade gift at Christmas. With each passing question, my parents dug deeper into the roots of our family, pulling out memories and events that were buried, as hidden treasure. They spoke of growing up in an era where cars were a luxury and the radio provided entertainment. The family would gather round and listen to favorite programs. They spoke of work-ethic, and what they were required to do around the home and community, a standard so different from today. They recounted the time of courting, and of their wedding day, held in a simple sanctuary with a reception in the church basement where guests drank punch and ate mints.

Nostalgia swept over me as I listened to stories of life in a simpler time and place. It explains so much about why my parents are the way they are, and how they came to be such extraordinary people. I asked my parents to give advice to their grandkids, and to share with them any wisdom they learned over their lifetimes. They encouraged the kids to find their passions and unique talents, to be honest people, and to stick together. The video is long, and every minute of it is deeply touching. It shows a couple of fifty years laughing, tearing up, sharing, and teaching. It is our living history.

As families, we gathered in a small room and watched it at Christmas. The comfort this video affords is immense, guaranteeing that these important stories will not be lost or forgotten. The mannerisms, interactions, voices, and smiles are all caught on the camera for everyone to enjoy for generations.

Capturing your heritage in video or audio is a beautiful and tangible way to preserve what is irreplaceable.

Here are interview questions in several categories from which to choose:

Your Beginning

- Names (do any of your names have special meaning or significance?)
- Birthplace, year
- Parents, where they were from
- Type of house you grew up in (size, conveniences, phones, etc.)
- Personalities of family members. Who were some of your special relatives?
- What is one of your earliest childhood memories?

Growing Up Years

- What schools did you attend?
- What kinds of games did you play? (at school and in the neighborhood)
- What was school like for you as a child?
- Were you involved in sports, music, drama, or other extra-curricular activities?
- What did you want to be when you grew up?
- Describe a typical family dinner.
- Did you have family chores? What were they? What was your least favorite?
- Any pets?
- Did you get an allowance? How much?
- How did your parents discipline you?
- Who were some of your most important friendships?

- Are there one to two stories that you remember clearly about your childhood?
- How much did you interact with your grandparents and other extended family?

The High School and College Years

- What was life like as a teenager?
- What were the fads from your youth? Hairstyles, clothing, music, etc.
- What was your favorite thing to do?
- What did teens do for fun? For dating?
- Did you play sports or participate in other activities?
- Did you drive a car? If so, what kind?
- Did you work?
- Where did you go to college?
- What was it like there?
- What did you study?

Courtship and Marriage

- How did you meet?
- What were your first impressions of each other?
- How did you propose? Did you ask the parents first?
- What memory stands out the most on your wedding day?
- What made you fall in love with _____? How did you know he/she was the one?
- What about the honeymoon?
- Where did you live?
- What was your first job? What was your boss like?
- What kinds of things did you do with your other married friends before kids?
- Did you serve in the military?

The Parenting Years

- Name your children. How did each one change your life?
- What did you do as a family that you thought was brilliant?
- What were some of the hard moments of parenting?
- What are some memories that stand out to you in the childrearing years?
- What advice would you give to parents today?
- How did you encourage relationships with your kids and their extended family?
- What are some of your proudest parenting moments?

The Empty Nest Years

- What was the hardest thing about kids leaving the nest?
- How did you adjust?
- What has been the best part of your post-parenting years?
- What advice would you give to parents heading into this season?
- What do you like about having grandkids?
- Special grandkid moments?
- What are some of your best grandparenting tips?
- What advice would you give to the grandkids? Or to individual grandkids?

Words of Wisdom

- What wisdom have you gained over a lifetime that you would like to share with the younger generation?
- Who were heroes to you?
- If you had to do something differently in your life, what would that be and why?
- What are you most grateful for?
- How has faith shaped and determined your life's journey?

- What is the key to a successful marriage?
- What is the key to successful parenting?
- What is something you want people to remember about you?

LEGACY dares

• Pull out an old family picture and talk to your kids about their heritage.

• Pick one area in which you'd like to improve the culture of your home. Do one action to make a positive impact in this moment.

• Think about one of the legacies you want to pass down. Do one small action to encourage that legacy today.

• Pick a family recipe to make for dinner tonight.

• Call a grandparent and find out the answer to one of the questions listed in the interview section.

Chapter 11

RECLAIMING FAITH

Now faith is confidence in what we hope for
and assurance in what we do not see.
–Hebrews 11:1 (NIV)

Faith is the strength by which a shattered world
shall emerge into the light.
–Helen Keller

We all have faith in something, whether it is our own abilities, our education, our heritage, our money, another person, our understanding of God, or a religious tradition. Sometimes when matters of faith are discussed, those who don't profess a belief in God feel left out of the conversation. In this chapter, I hope you will join me in thinking through how the spiritual realm can be part of reclaiming home. Faith makes a pivotal difference in my family, offering hope, guidance, and perspective. Sometimes becoming parents causes people to think more deeply about their own beliefs and assumptions about the big questions in life. I invite you to join me in a faith conversation in this chapter.

One year in my twenties, I went on a backpacking trip in the Superstition Wilderness in Arizona. This is a desert area filled with hundreds of acres of dry, desolate, barren mountains. Very little water exists there. Loaded with heavy packs, we trekked in, traveling a significant distance each day. On the third day, it began to rain. When it didn't stop, we made the decision to set up camp on a bank next to a small creek. I remember sitting in my tent watching the rain pelt the hard, red clay. It was as if the soil had a protective barrier that didn't allow the rain to penetrate. The water would splash hard on the ground and run quickly off, leaving a snakelike trail behind.

By the following day, it was clear that the rain was not going to stop. Problematically, all of our gear was getting soaked. Some people in our group were not prepared for the change in weather. One guy bought his hiking boots in the men's shoe department at Nordstrom—not exactly the rugged wear designed to keep the feet dry. He and a couple of others were beginning to show signs of hypothermia. The creek, so small the day before, was now a river too deep to cross. We had camped on the opposite side of the river from the trail that led out to safety. Flash floods were beginning and we were stuck in the wilderness.

Splitting up, those of us who were able went looking for a protected place to camp at a higher elevation, away from the rising water. We knew we had to work quickly. Our friends needed to get warm, and it wouldn't be long before the rest of us would be in trouble too. Scrambling up steep rocks and ledges, we searched. At one point, I stopped and leaned against a rock. My clothes dripped, saturated, and the sheets of rain clouded my vision. "Lord!" I prayed silently, *"we need help."*

I breathed deeply, summoning courage, and circled to the right around the outcropping against which I'd been leaning. Not fifty feet away, high in the cliff, was a cave. My heart beating fast, I called to my friend and together we climbed up the scree slope. It wasn't just a cave. It was an ancient cave *dwelling* built by the Salado Indians over six hundred years ago. There were three levels, plenty of room for the entire group, and dry firewood that someone had left. We set up a kitchen, a sleeping area, and a gear-drying station next to the fire.

For the next four days, we watched from our perch as rain penetrated the once resistant clay. The parched earth yielded to the downpour, and the entire desert floor was transformed into a rushing river basin.

Our souls sometimes mirror that hard, baked desert clay. Living in a culture of distraction and abundance, we give ourselves to shallow pursuits day after day, and our souls become hard, rigid, and protected. Staying in the superficial keeps us from the meaningful, deep, heart places of soulful living. The result of this shallow living is a life left wanting and unfulfilled.

In *Renovation of the Heart*, Dallas Willard writes, "Fundamental aspects of life, art, sleep, sex, ritual, family, parenting, community, health, and meaningful work are all soul functions; they fail and fall apart to the degree that the soul diminishes. When we speak of the human soul we are speaking of the deepest level of life and power in the human being ... and the very first thing that we must do is to be mindful of our soul, to acknowledge it. It is necessary to take the soul seriously and deal with it regularly and intelligently."

The concept that Willard describes is that whether we recognize it or not, our soul is in the driver's seat of our life and the condition of it determines whether we travel well or crash and burn. King David, one of the most memorable figures in history, wrote, "You, God, are my God, earnestly I seek you; I thirst for you, my *whole being* longs for you, in a dry and parched land where there is no water." (Psalms 63:1, NIV)

Here is the problem, all of us, parents and kids alike, look for something to fill our souls: family, friendships, education, prestige, achievements, sports, beauty, etc. We think to ourselves, "*This* is going to make me happy!" And for a while it might ... but it doesn't last. Though those things listed are *all good*, they can't fill the deepest place of the soul that is reserved for the spiritual. Our souls are built to contain God, but when we fill them with other things, there is no room.

King David had power, a position of authority, great wealth, athletic prowess, and beautiful women. Yet, it all came up short and he longed for his God. This longing isn't just for heroes of the faith. Our friend, Ryan, described his experience winning the Super Bowl in the NFL. He said, "I played football my entire childhood, building up to this one moment. It was the pinnacle of my life. Yet, as I looked around, I thought, *Is this all there is? Is this it?*" Winning the Super Bowl was amazing, but it didn't *fill* him like he thought it would. Like Ryan and King David, at some point we come to the realization that nothing will fill that soul-space adequately, except the one who created it.

Our souls are the dwelling place of God. There is an inherent yearning for God's love, grace, acceptance, forgiveness, and mercy. Tending to this relationship will have untold benefits, both for you personally, and in your family. It provides a place of safety and protection when the floods come and threaten to wash us away. When we do give our spiritual life attention, like the baked, red clay saturated under the water, the soil of our inner life softens. We set an anchor to something bigger than our own selves.

Growing in our spiritual mindset helps us understand the sacredness of the world and of life itself. It points to the joy that comes from a compassionate heart and generous living. Faith offers a confidence that bad situations can be redeemed for good, and the belief that there is a purpose and a plan for every individual alive. Perhaps most importantly, having a spiritual perspective offers hope in a world that can be discouraging and painful. Most parents desire for their children to grab hold of these positive truths, and weaving the spiritual realm into their lives will help shape this worldview.

As parents, we need this inner investment, and so do our children. This pursuit requires breathing room—a *slowing down*. It begs for walks in the woods, hours without media, and time connecting in a faith community. In our culture we have glorified busy. Busy somehow means significant. Who made this up and why have we bought into it? Why do we often feel twinges of guilt when we have free space in our lives? Busy actually can mean burnt out and distracted. How often has this pace of life robbed our joy, stolen our precious minutes, and left us ragged? Most tragically, busyness and distraction have washed away depth of soul.

Look at the world in which our kids live. There is a significant emphasis on various types of media, fashion trends, sexuality, and peer conformity. They could spend their entire childhood engrossed in virtual lives and images that prevent them from going to the deeper places of their souls. This is the world in which we live. It's not going away, so we have to find ways to counter the superficial habits.

Whatever your spiritual views, it is logical to conclude that a noisy lifestyle does not lead to inner peace. Cultivating spirituality requires that we make room for it. God does not shout, he quietly whispers. If our children will not take it upon themselves to carve out this spiritual white space, we, as parents, need to create it for them. While we cannot control their spiritual journey, we can expose them to experiences and environments that allow an opportunity for God to take residence in their lives. So how do parents organize family life to make room for soul care and spiritual renewal?

EXPLORE YOUR OWN FAITH VIEWS

It is difficult to pass on something you don't possess yourself. Take the time to cultivate your own faith journey. For many people this starts with considering their own spiritual heritage and deciding if they want to focus there, or to explore other beliefs. Some people have been wounded by others in the name of God and this clouds their perspective regarding spiritual issues. If this is the case for you, consider how you can focus on the core of faith, rather than on the people who may have caused harm. Join a study group at the church you attend, find a spiritual friend and read a book together, pray often, or set aside a few minutes every morning to read scripture. When we center our souls on the spiritual, we spill more kindness, love, patience, and self-control. These traits are attractive to our children. They are more likely to want to learn about faith if they are seeing positive characteristics, as a result of faith, in their parents.

DEMONSTRATE LOVE

I once heard someone say that how a child views a parent will often shape their view of God. This has certainly been true in my own life. Because of my dad, I have no trouble picturing a loving, generous, kind, and strong Father in heaven. The sincere compassion and love you show to your children provides the foundation on which they can accept and experience God's love.

Einstein said, "The most important question a person can ask is, 'Is the Universe a friendly place?'" The answer to this question will, in large part, be determined by how our children experience genuine love and care in our homes. This has direct impact on their worldview, especially spiritually.

TALK ABOUT SPIRITUALITY

Teaching our children to love God begins with conversations about him. When your daughter picks up a caterpillar on a walk, you talk about a God who is creative enough to make that creature. When your son brings home homework that discusses what elements combine in order for earth to sustain humankind, you talk about the One who placed all of nature systematically to flourish. Discussing God becomes a normal part of daily living.

There is a passage in the book of Deuteronomy that describes this phenomenon beautifully, "Place these words {of God} on your hearts. Get them deep inside you. Tie them on your hands and foreheads as a reminder. Teach them to your children. Talk about them wherever you are, sitting at home or walking in the street; talk about them from the time you get up in the morning until you fall into bed at night." (Deuteronomy11:18-19, MSG)

We do not need to feel the burden of having explanations to all questions about God and the universe. The point is to simply have those deeper conversations. We get to explore this profound and mysterious part of us together.

INCORPORATE PRAYER

The biggest questions about prayer are: what is prayer, to whom are we praying, and why is it important?

Prayer is, at its essence, something remarkably simple, and yet, simultaneously, complex and mysterious. It is a conversation. A friendship. Prayer is both speaking and listening to God. C. S. Lewis wrote that there is always a conversation happening between our deepest self and our creator. Prayer is just tuning into the conversation already happening.

Prayer is also deeply personal. Some prefer to pray in a building with intricate stained glass and formal pews. Others find the woods or mountaintop to be their sanctuary that nourishes prayer. It doesn't matter much where we pray, but that it becomes a regular part of our inner life. Indeed, **all of life can become an act of prayer and worship.** The more integrated we become spiritually in our lives, the more we will experience this congruency.

When we pray, we acknowledge that there is something more than what we see on this earth. You may call this being something else, but I call him *Immanuel*, God with us. Prayer is simply cultivating a relationship with God by offering praise, a surrendered heart, communication, gratitude, and worship. The nature of this relationship is safe. I know my God to be trustworthy, faithful, loving, kind, and generous. Therefore, when I pray, I am free to offer up what is in my heart to him.

Prayer is important because it changes us. Oswald Chambers writes, "Prayer is the way that the life of God in us is nourished." It requires a posture of humility, and an open heart. When we pray we search our hearts for offenses that need correction, and we find grace. We are given the power to forgive, and we are able to present our requests to God, letting go of control. Most importantly, prayer allows us to get to know God himself. It changes our perspective about the situations in our lives, and allows us to see from a new lens.

Prayer is a spiritual practice that awakens our souls. It tethers us to the one who breathes life into those deep places.

My friend, Rychelle, a chaplain, describes how she encourages patients to use "breath prayers." These are simple expressions that communicate the deepest cries of the heart. They are simple, short, and spoken throughout the day. When a patient is in pain, for example, he may not have the strength or mental clarity to say a prayer. But what he can do is offer a breath prayer, asking for peace or calm in the midst of discomfort.

Picture the rhythm of breath prayers, breathing out your need to God, then inhaling his power to sustain you. These prayers work for the powerless, the busy, the slammed, and the overwhelmed. They work in crisis, and they work when life is bountiful. They are beneficial for those new to prayer, and for those who have prayed for years. The point is not to become "good" at prayer, but to engage God in the most authentic way possible in whatever stage or life circumstance in which you find yourself.

Prayer can be woven into the routine of your family's life. Sometimes you may utter breath prayers together, sometimes they may be read out of a book, other times you may bow in silence. The more you pray, the more natural it becomes.

Pray at the dinner table, pray when you drive your kids to school, pray when life is good, and pray when life is hard. Prayer requires moments of quiet. Create those windows, no matter how small.

PRIORITIZE QUIETUDE

I love the word "quietude." Do you know what it means? It's the state of being quiet; tranquility; calmness. How does this sound to you? Probably to most of us overscheduled, stressed parents, it sounds great! There is very little quietude in my busy home. Most of us parents live in a space where it is difficult to hear our own thoughts, let alone the voice of God. Children do not have the same appreciation for quiet as adults, but it is still important for their souls to experience quietude on a regular basis. We can help them build this into their lives by walking in the woods, having morning quiet time with books or a kid's Bible, limiting media use, curbing overscheduled calendars, getting outside, and turning off noise in our homes.

COMMIT TO A FAITH COMMUNITY

Pausing in the week to go to a place designated for spiritual growth communicates that you value spending time learning about God, and that it is worth the sacrifice of time. With a little bit of work you should be able to find a trusted place of worship that feels comfortable for your family. Churches today offer a wide variety of worship styles, doctrinal stances, and atmospheres. It is easy to become lazy about church attendance. After all, when our lives are so busy, we may prefer a slow morning in our pajamas. I can relate—this is true in many seasons of our year.

Even so, part of reclaiming faith means we order our lives differently. It means we say with our time, *this is important and worth the sacrifice.* I have a friend who did not take the time to go to church when her children were young. "We were too busy, and we were always so tired," she said. Now, she deeply regrets that decision. My friend's children, now adults, do not see the importance of going to church, either for themselves or for their children. No matter how hard my friend tries to persuade them, they won't take her grandchildren to church.

Cultural norms can easily overtake our time and our values, so we have to be intentional about holding fast to the main things and paring back on others. For example, why is it that we won't dream of missing a soccer game, but church is optional? I ask that for myself more than anyone as we navigate three children though club soccer teams who have games every day of the week. It's a question to be pondered. It is important we take a hard look at how we've allowed culture to tell us what is important and what matters. Taking our family to church creates space for the spiritual and communicates values.

Another benefit of being a part of a faith community is that it nurtures relationships with people who will also care about your children. Church family will often invest in their lives, and give your kids a sense of extended family. This is another way for your tribe to experience deep roots in a place.

FIND A SPIRITUAL YOUTH ORGANIZATION

At every stage of development, our children benefit from having spiritual input from people outside of their family. When my husband was in ninth grade, his basketball coach was a Young Life leader. Young Life is a non-denominational Christian outreach that informally claims, "It's a sin to bore kids with the gospel." So they don't. They make living the Christian life wildly fun, exciting, and meaningful. It proved to be lifechanging for my husband, who was hanging around with a crowd that was not leading him in a positive direction. He learned about faith in God, and it set his life on a course from which he has never turned back.

Whether you find a youth group, a spiritual mentor, or a small circle of friends, encouraging faith in your children through others is important. Your children benefit from having stable people in their lives who genuinely care about them as people, and who want to support them through life's ups and downs. This is especially true in the often tumultuous teen years, where teens are sometimes more likely to listen to a youth leader than a parent.

BE A BLESSING

Every day when my kids leave the house, I say, *"Be blessed and be a blessing."* This means *do something today to impact your world for good.* It doesn't matter what. It can be sharpening a classmate's pencil, encouraging a friend, or standing up for someone who needs help. It also means, receive the gifts God has *already* given in your life. Express gratitude as you consider the blessings God has poured out.

When we are kind to others, give of ourselves in service, or choose patience over anger, we are a blessing. This attitude turns the me-centered child inside out. It is good for all of us to put our faith to action. It makes it real in our lives.

Five days after I prayed that prayer in the Superstition Wilderness, the floods decreased enough that we could make our way out of the desert. The clay stuck to our boots, no longer hard. Our trip had turned out so much differently than expected. When we planned our route and packed our bags, there was no way to predict the situation that ensued. The cave had been our lifesaver, literally.

Faith in God is much like that cave. Our lives will veer off course and we will experience sudden storms. Our faith provides a safe place where we can find rest, peace, and sanctuary. It invites us to grab hold of *hope*. What better gift could we offer ourselves and our children?

RECLAIMING FAITH
dares

• Read one Bible verse to your kids today and discuss.

• Pray out loud, as a family, over a pressing situation.

• Put on contemporary inspirational music, or hymns, throughout the day.

• Decide, as a family, on a church to attend, or a youth organization to try.

• Ask your children, "How can you be a blessing today, and how have you been blessed?"

CONCLUSION

Every fall I stand and stare at the bags of bulbs in the garden center. My heart longs for the delicate spring flowers pictured on the front of the bag, but my mind thinks about how much work it's going to be to get out in the cold weather and plant them. Bulbs have to be planted with the long term in mind. Summer flowers offer instant gratification as we bring them home and see our pots transformed into glorious shouts of color in an instant. Spring bulbs take effort and time. More often than not, I repress my lazy side, and grab a bag.

Using my bulb planter, I dig deeply into the soil and lay the rock-like bulb in the ground. I wonder, with each hole, how something so lifeless and hard can produce such beauty in the spring. For months and months, over long winters with deep snow, there is no apparent movement. Yet, that cold dormant period is the very element that stimulates root development in the bulb. Without it, the bulb would not bloom. Then, as if by total surprise, exclaiming the grand entrance of spring to the world, the fresh green leaves shoot through the thawing ground. Those spring flowers, planted in hope, bring a burst of joy to our souls after a long winter. I realize then that my effort was worth it; my small investment to plant yields surprisingly beautiful results.

Isn't that just like our journey with our families? We fight laziness. It's a lot of work to plant. And even when we do, we often don't see results for a long season of winter. I've been there and I *am* there. Day after day planting, planting, planting, hoping for the spring bloom, yet not seeing those green shoots quite yet. Just head-down, digging holes. I am often tempted to throw my shovel down and stop planting. It can be so discouraging and disheartening to plant without visible results. But my hope does not falter because of the absence, because I know that the dormant season is a necessary part of growing roots.

Let's be seasoned gardeners as we tend to the soil of our families. Let's plant patiently and abundantly, each small act performed with the hope of a future blossom. Some days our planting is an ordinary task such as packing lunches. Some days we may put a generous meal on the table for the family to enjoy. Other days it means we set aside social media to connect with the hearts of our children. Sometimes we make room to go on the date with our spouse that we've been talking about for months. Or we set aside activities and sit at the feet of grandparents, soaking in their stories and presence. Planting abundantly ultimately means in all of our actions—we practice and sow in love, acceptance, communication, play, and presence. It means we don't give up—we keep planting, each and every day. The results will not be immediately evident as roots are slowly growing. In fact, the blooms may take years to show themselves, but that doesn't mean they won't come.

The other day I heard a man talk about the prayers and acts of faithfulness of his grandmother. He was bent on rebellion and hard living, abusing both people and substances. But his small, yet strong-hearted grandma welcomed him into her home, her life, and her prayers, every single day. Ultimately, this steadfast loyalty and love was the catalyst that turned his life around. Imagine how that grandmother felt when she finally saw the small green shoots in the thawing heart of that man. I'm sure there were no words that could adequately describe the joy. Like this grandmother, we, too, trust that little by little by little, with each planting, there is a flower preparing to bloom.

When we get weary with the small acts, or our days get hard, when there is no single sign of life, we must remind each other that spring is coming. That is the beautiful part of community. That is what we can do for each other. My friend started a community garden at a local school. She designates a different person for each raised bed. That individual is responsible for her particular box, but all help one another and partake in the bounty of the harvest. This is a beautiful picture of what we can be for one another. We each tend to our own, but we help one another when there is extra work, and we all share in the ownership of the garden. Find your small group of fellow gardeners who are also digging, planting, and hoping as they reclaim their families. Is one of them discouraged? Remind them. Is there someone who needs help finding purpose in the ordinary, or in reclaiming time, or any of the other areas of reclaiming family? Help them. Then celebrate with one another when the harvest comes.

Strong roots grow because someone did the hard work of planting. You are strong enough to plant, dear friend. Be strong inwardly. Don't give up hope. No one else will do the work—your family—your marriage—needs YOU. Believe it, and then strike the shovel, knowing that you are the difference maker. What you say and do matters. It matters to your children most of all, but it also permeates the world. You impact those you raise, and then the ripples reach far beyond your grasp, stretching into generations. You are a leader; your influence sets your family on a course for good. The daily actions that seem so small add up to strong roots that create the very foundation on which children stand forever.

Never forget who you are: life changer. You are courageous. Strong, brave, steady. Able to look challenges in the face with the unbending determination of a parent, one of the strongest forces in the world. Imperfection is your friend. It reveals the beauty of authentic humanity and makes room for humility and do-overs. You live by the truth that *love* holds all things together and base your life on that principle. You are comforter—providing shelter from fierce storms. You lock arms with hope, the sustainer, who never, ever gives up. You set a firm anchor. Unshakeable. You are brave and fierce enough to RECLAIM HOME!

YOU ARE A *difference maker.*

You impact those you raise, and the ripples
reach far beyond your grasp, stretching into generations.

YOU ARE A *leader*

your influence setting your family on a course for good. The
daily actions that seem so small add up to deep roots that
form the foundation on which children stand forever.

you live by the truth that L♥VE
holds all things together & that
L · O · V · E · W · I · N · S

YOU ARE *courageous*
··——≫ STRONG, BRAVE, STEADY. ≪——··
You root your family in the soil of
love, acceptance, play, communication & presence.

YOU ARE *comforter*
- sheltering from strong winds & storms.
You lock arms with hope, the sustainer.

NEVER FORGET WHO YOU ARE :

life changer

UNSHAKEABLE. ≪——≫ UNSTOPPABLE.

You are brave and fierce enough to
RECLAIM HOME.

ABOUT THE AUTHOR

Krista Gilbert is an author, blogger, and speaker who lives in the mountains of Idaho with her husband, Erik, and their four children. Passionate about bringing meaning and fun to the table, she inspires others to live their lives on purpose—encouraging deep roots of connection, faith, love, and grace. When she isn't blogging at kristagilbert.com, or daring families at meaninginaminute.com, you will find her dancing around the kitchen cooking, laughing wholeheartedly, or racing her kids down a ski run.

APPENDIX

CHAPTER 4: RECLAIMING MARRIAGE

Recommended Resources:

Jhranch.com—an adventure camp for wives and husbands. They also offer parent/child camps

Meaninginaminute.com—the marriage dare; or twelve dates in twelve months

Sacred Marriage—a book by Gary Thomas

Familylife.com—a website designed to support couples and families

The Family Life Marriage Conference—a branch of familylife.com

Love and Respect—a book by Emerson Eggerichs

iMarriage—a CD or DVD study by Andy Stanley

Sheet Music—a book by Dr. Kevin Leman

CHAPTER 5: RECLAIMING CHILDHOOD

Recommended Resources:

Campspalding.org—an activity driven Christian camp for kids of all ages

Commonsensemedia.org—this website is specifically designed to improve the lives of kids and families by providing the trustworthy information, education, and independent voice they need to thrive in a world of media and technology.

Internet-safety.yoursphere.com—a website designed to help parents navigate internet safety.

Covenant Eyes—an Internet filtering software

Pluggedin.com—a movie review website

Rottentomatoes.com—a movie review website

(These resources were current at time of publication, but online resources are subject to change.)

CHAPTER 8: RECLAIMING THE TABLE

My version of "cooking group" makes twelve meals to take home for each person. The menu includes savory marinades, delicious, healthy sauces, and even gluten-free dishes. Here are the basic nuts and bolts:

1. Pick three friends who want to cook with you.
2. Designate a "buyer" for the month. One person plans and buys for the group that month.
3. Everyone comes prepared with an apron, a labeled cooler, a knife, cutting board, and mixing bowl.
4. Each cook takes a recipe and gets to work.
5. The planner passes out a list of the meals and the cooking directions for each.

6. The final grocery bill is divided by the number of people in the group, and each person pays the buyer.
7. Take the meals home, fill your freezer, and enjoy the satisfaction of having these delicious meals on hand!

A few of my all-time favorite recipes:

Blackberry/Huckleberry BBQ Sauce

Where we live, huckleberries are a tradition and a treasure.

1 1/2 cups blackberries or huckleberries (or a combination of both)
1/3 cup ketchup
1/3 cup honey
1/4 cup brown sugar
1/4 cup minced ginger
2 cloves garlic
1 1/2 teaspoons pepper
1-2 teaspoons hot sauce or red chili flakes

Combine all ingredients in a blender or food processor. Mix well. Place in a saucepan and cook down until the flavors combine. Serve with any meat.

Soft Peanut Brittle

The Davenport is an historic hotel in Spokane, WA, where I grew up. They have been making soft peanut brittle for years and are famous for it. You'll love it. Here's my version:

2 cups creamy peanut butter
1 1/2 cups sugar
1 1/2 cups light corn syrup

1/4 cup water + 2 teaspoons

2 1/2 tablespoons butter

2 cups peanuts

1 teaspoon baking soda

1 teaspoon vanilla extract

Put well-greased baking sheets, or slabs of marble in the freezer so that they get very cold.

Dissolve the baking soda in 2 teaspoons water and set aside.

In a double boiler, soften the peanut butter. Meanwhile, boil the sugar, corn syrup, and 1/4 cup water until it reaches 275 degrees on a candy thermometer. When it reaches that temperature, lower the heat to medium and add the butter. Add peanuts and cook for six more minutes, or until the thermometer reaches 300 degrees. Take off the heat and add the dissolved baking soda and vanilla. Fold in the warm peanut butter and mix gently.

Pour the mixture onto the cold cookie sheets and spread thin (working quickly). The secret of this candy is quick cooling, so the cold baking sheets help. The Davenport uses marble.

Break into pieces and enjoy!

K.G.'s Vanilla Zucchini Bread

We are zucchini bread crazy in our family and this recipe beats all.

1 teaspoon baking soda

1 teaspoon salt

1/2 teaspoon baking powder

3 teaspoons cinnamon

3 cups flour

2 cups sugar

1 cup oil

3 eggs

3 tablespoons vanilla (yes, tablespoons, it's not a misprint)

2 1/2 cups shredded zucchini

Mix the wet ingredients together in a mixer and blend. Mix the dry ingredients in a bowl. Slowly add to the wet ingredients. Pour into a greased loaf pan. Bake at 325 degrees for 45-60 minutes, or until a toothpick comes out clean in the center.

CHAPTER 9: RECLAIMING TRADITIONS

Hootenanny Caramel Corn

This is our annual party recipe that I got from an Amish woman in Lancaster County years ago.

8 quarts popped popcorn

2 cups brown sugar

1/2 cup corn syrup

1 teaspoon vanilla

1 cup butter

1 teaspoon salt

1/2 teaspoon soda

Boil sugar, butter, corn syrup, and salt for five minutes. Remove from heat. Add soda and vanilla. Pour over popcorn and bake at 250 degrees for one hour. Stir occasionally.

How to Host a Hootenanny:

1. Invite friends to a fall harvest party, telling them to bring soup, chili, or dessert for a cook-off, and a pumpkin to decorate.

2. Set out tables with power strips for the crockpots. Designate a place for desserts.

3. When people arrive, they check in at registration. There, they write the name of their soup or chili on a bowl, and their name on the bottom of the bowl. This gets taped to their crockpot. They write the name of their soup on a tag and put it in front of their entry. If they have a dessert entry, they write the name of their dessert on a tag and their name on the inside.

4. The preselected judges fill the bowls with soup or chili and take the bowls to a judging table. They pick the winners (dessert judges are doing this at that time also).

5. Meanwhile, there are potato sack races, apple bobbing, tug-of-wars, three-legged races, and egg tosses going on.

6. After the judging, everyone eats.

7. Try to find some 4-H students to bring their rabbits to your party for a petting zoo.

8. Announce the winners and give prizes for the cook-off.

9. Decorate pumpkins using glue guns and woodland objects.

10. Take pictures and enjoy celebrating autumn!

Empty Tomb Biscuits

This is a great recipe for Easter morning with kids.

1 package refrigerated crescent rolls
1 bag large marshmallows
1/2 cup butter, melted
3/4 cup sugar
2 tablespoons cinnamon

Preheat oven to 350 degrees and grease a muffin tin. Place the melted butter in a bowl. Place the cinnamon and sugar in another bowl. Separate the crescent rolls into triangles. Place a large marshmallow in each one. Seal the edges of the roll around each marshmallow. Roll the dough in your hands to form a smooth circle. Dip the dough in melted butter, then in the cinnamon sugar mixture. Place each roll in the greased muffin tin. Bake for fifteen minutes. Allow the tombs to cool. Kids open the tombs to see they are empty!

ACKNOWLEDGMENTS

I can't possibly detail every person who has been a part of rooting me in this life, so I will recognize those who have directly impacted the content of this book or my writing journey.

To my God—I look around and see that the boundary lines have fallen for me in pleasant places, that I have the most beautiful inheritance by virtue of Your grace. It is all from You, God. Your faithfulness has been present and evident in each and every day that I have lived. May my response always be one of praise to You, and service to Your people.

To Erik—your strength, depth, humor, insight, and love root us. We are who we are as a family because of your integrity and commitment. I am so thankful that our children swing from your unbending branches. Thank you for being my rock and my soft place to land. Growing old with you is the best.

To McKenna, Dawson, Hudson, and Stetson—this book is written for you. This is your heritage and your story as much as it is mine. I hold many titles in this life, but none more important than "Mom." Each of you sets a most unique place at our family table. You all make up this crazy, imperfect, and beautiful group that we call our family. I am privileged and honored beyond measure to get to be *your* mama. I love you with my whole heart and soul!

To Mom and Dad—your small, everyday actions and words created the firm foundation on which I now stand. Though I will never fully understand why I was the one born into this family, I overflow with gratitude every single day of my life. You are the best kind of people on this earth.

To Kendra and Mitch—siblings are the only ones in this world who travel with you from start to finish. I couldn't ask for better friends and traveling companions. You both have shaped who I am, and who I've become. I admire you, respect you, and love you beyond words. Eric and Sarah, you have been the perfect completion of our family circle. To say I am grateful is an understatement. You all mean the absolute world to me.

To Grandma and Grandpa Thomas and Grandma Jones—you taught me what it means to build a legacy and establish a home. Your ripples are felt every day... and I miss you terribly.

To my nieces and nephews—Gabe, Caleb, Olivia, Maddie, Zoe, Gwyneth, Brita, Jo, Kat, and Kara—individually, you are amazing. Together we create something special. Cousins are the best kinds of friends.

To the Gilberts—thank you for welcoming me into your adventurous clan, and for your example of sacrificial love, dedication, and commitment to family.

To my extended family—you have always been my cheerleaders and my people. I'm so grateful for the role each of you plays in our family tree, and in my life.

To Katie—you have been my family since we met in third grade. Your fingerprints are all over the pages of this book. You are the friend God gave me to show His faithfulness. When I'm with you, it's like coming home.

To Alex—you are both my soul friend and my advisor. I'm so grateful for our history, our shared passions, and for our commitment to each other's families. Thank you for being the one who challenges, encourages, and sharpens me on this writing journey. You and Derek are gold.

To Tammy and Karin—thank you for being my oak-tree people. Our roots have grown deeply together. We belong to each other, and it is so good. Our circle of friendship is a true gift, and a source of encouragement and strength. God had definite plans when he moved us close to one another! Our cord of three strands is strong and enduring.

To Rychelle, Connie, Jill, and Andrea—you all have a way of making people feel valued and loved at just the right moment. Thank you for speaking life to me when I needed it most, and for being the kind of people who inspire me by the way you live. You are all women of faith and character, and it is a privilege to do life together.

To Rebecca, Mandy, and Kerri—we cut our parenting teeth together in the formative early years. Those hours we spent shaped who I am as a parent today. I continue to be inspired and sharpened by the way you do family and life. You live extraordinary lives.

To my cooking group (Kristi, Angie, and Zetta)—you save my sanity! Stirring pots and sharing laughter and tears is a beautiful display of encouragement and community in my life. I treasure you, and am grateful that we share a table.

To Camp Spalding—you have created a spiritual home for my children and for me. We are a different family because of our time spent there.

To Carla Foote—you were my godsend in this season. Thank you for your tireless efforts to make this book the best that it could be. You are an amazing editor, and a beautiful soul.

To Crystal of newshopdesign.com—you work tirelessly to bring the best results possible to our projects. You have been one of the greatest gifts on this writing/blogging journey. I'd be lost without you! Thank you for your faithful service, and for pushing the envelope with me.

To Mary Darr—thank you for being my last-minute rescue. I am so grateful!

To Terry Whalin—thank you for seeing potential in me.

Writing this book has been an act of God's grace in my life, and only because of His faithfulness do I have anything to say at all. Every step of this journey has been covered in prayer. While writing this book, Ephesians 3:16-19 (NIV) has been rooted in my soul, and that is the scripture I now pray for you as we close:

*"I pray that out of his glorious riches he may strengthen you with power through His Spirit in your inner being, so that Christ may dwell in your hearts through faith. And I pray that you, **being rooted and established in love**, may have power, together with all of the Lord's holy people, to grasp how wide and long and high and deep is the love of Christ, and to know this love that surpasses knowledge—that you may be filled to the measure of all the fullness of God."*